Consumer Affairs

Independence Educational Publishers

First published by Independence Educational Publishers

The Studio, High Green

Great Shelford

Cambridge CB22 5EG

England

© Independence 2019

Copyright

Photocopy licence

ISBN-13: 978 1 86168 801 9

Printed in Great Britain

Zenith Print Group

Contents

Introduction

CONSUMER AFFAIRS is Volume 345 in the **ISSUES** series. The aim of the series is to offer current, diverse information about important issues in our world, from a UK perspective.

ABOUT CONSUMER AFFAIRS

In recent years the way we behave as consumers has changed drastically. The increasing preference by consumers to shop online has had a devastating effect on the high street with more and more big brands in crisis or disappearing altogether. This book looks at current consumer trends, consumer rights and how 'conscious consumerism' is on the rise, particularly among milennials.

OUR SOURCES

Titles in the **ISSUES** series are designed to function as educational resource books, providing a balanced overview of a specific subject.

The information in our books is comprised of facts, articles and opinions from many different sources, including:

⇨ Newspaper reports and opinion pieces

⇨ Website factsheets

⇨ Magazine and journal articles

⇨ Statistics and surveys

⇨ Government reports

⇨ Literature from special interest groups.

A NOTE ON CRITICAL EVALUATION

Because the information reprinted here is from a number of different sources, readers should bear in mind the origin of the text and whether the source is likely to have a particular bias when presenting information (or when conducting their research). It is hoped that, as you read about the many aspects of the issues explored in this book, you will critically evaluate the information presented.

It is important that you decide whether you are being presented with facts or opinions. Does the writer give a biased or unbiased report? If an opinion is being expressed, do you agree with the writer? Is there potential bias to the 'facts' or statistics behind an article?

ASSIGNMENTS

In the back of this book, you will find a selection of assignments designed to help you engage with the articles you have been reading and to explore your own opinions. Some tasks will take longer than others and there is a mixture of design, writing and research-based activities that you can complete alone or in a group.

Useful weblinks

www.asa.org.uk

www.black-friday.global

www.cada.co.uk

www.ethicalconsumer.org

www.ethicalhour.co.uk

www.fairtrade.org.uk

www.fashionunited.uk

www.globalactionplan.org.uk

www.greenfunders.org

www.independent.co.uk

www.inews.co.uk

www.itgovernance.co.uk

www.mintel.com

www.mygov.scot

www.ons.gov.uk

www.oxfam.org.uk

www.retail-insight-network.com

www.smartinsights.com

www.theconversation.com

www.theguardian.com

FURTHER RESEARCH

At the end of each article we have listed its source and a website that you can visit if you would like to conduct your own research. Please remember to critically evaluate any sources that you consult and consider whether the information you are viewing is accurate and unbiased.

Chapter 1

Consumer trends

Mintel announces six new trends shaping the global consumer landscape

Mintel has revealed six key consumer trends impacting industries and markets around the world and identified how they will play out in the years to come. In 2019 and beyond, the global consumer landscape will evolve like never before, driven by themes of privacy, individuality, wellness, convenience and connectivity:

- **Total wellbeing:** Consumers are treating their bodies like an ecosystem and seeking solutions that complement their personal health and evolving needs.

- **Challenge accepted:** A growing momentum to take on new challenges is driving consumers to reach new heights and uncover new passions.

- **Rethink plastic:** While not inherently bad, the throwaway use of plastic is driving consumers to review their own behaviours to prevent plastic pollution.

- **On display:** Consumers and brands are becoming more aware that they have a digital persona to nurture and grow, creating tension as everyone fights for attention and nobody is safe from scrutiny.

- **Social isolation:** Constant digital connectivity, where physical interactions are replaced with digital updates, can increase feelings of loneliness, social isolation and depression, creating a demand for products and services that help consumers learn to disconnect.

- **Redefining adulthood:** The concept of what it means to be an adult has changed beyond recognition and consumers are adapting to lives that don't fit the mould.

Here, the global Mintel Trends analyst team explores how these trends are set to shake up markets around the world, including implications for both consumers and brands.

Total wellbeing

In 2019 and beyond, growing consumer curiosity with the microbiome shows no signs of abating. From gut-friendly fermented foods to probiotic skincare, consumers will demand products that balance and boost the natural bacteria found in and on the body.

Consumers are looking externally to their surroundings and internally towards their physical and mental wellbeing, expecting holistic approaches to wellness. Across the globe consumers are increasingly seeking personalisation and in the UK, as many as 42% of British consumers are interested in a personalised diet based on their genes/DNA.

Developments in health monitoring, such as skin sensors or ingestible capsules, will satisfy consumers' demand for this personalised approach, while also building on scientific research in these emerging fields.

Challenge accepted

As appetites for adventure grow, consumers are becoming more willing than ever to expand their comfort zones, push themselves to the limit with new experiences and use social media to compete with and offer inspiration to their peers.

Social media inspiration is blurring the line between reality and lifegoals, opening consumers up to a whole new world. In fact, a third (32%) of Canadian consumers who have attended a live event say they learn about live events from social media. It may be fuelling a love of adventure, but social media is not without its pitfalls and in the years to come, companies and brands should proceed with caution.

Rethink plastic

When it comes to recycling, well-meaning consumers are desperate to do the right thing but often simply don't know how or where to start. As consumers continue to challenge brands over the perils of plastic waste, the development of recyclable products and packaging that are convenient for consumers to separate will be critical. But equally as important will be creating incentives and initiatives; in China, 58% of Mintropolitans* are willing to pay more for ethical brands.

In 2019 and beyond, expect to see more sponsored 'reverse' vending machines and bring your-own-mug schemes. But it takes more than any one individual or brand to save the world; the future will be about working together. Companies and organisations should look to partner in order to create or crowdsource ideas that will make innovative and disruptive changes, such as the development of biodegradable materials, the search to enhance the recyclability of plastic or the cultivation of a better waste management system.

On display

Consumers and brands have come to accept and nurture their digital personas, perfectly curating their online identities. But even among the most carefully crafted feeds, one misguided post can lead to intense scrutiny and public backlash. In the US, 16% of Hispanic social media users have boycotted brands based on things they learned on social media.

Now more than ever, it's crucial for companies and brands to have social media strategies in place and to train employees about company morals and etiquette, so that when (not if) they are faced with a sensitive issue, they know how to handle it in a timely way. While it is important to balance the cycle of 'negative exposure' by sharing good, positive stories, it's equally important to promote critical thinking and dissent. This will help brands align with consumers' defiant side and break through their filter bubbles.

Social isolation

Technology can make the world a lonely place. Consumers increasingly live their lives through smartphone screens and, although connected electronically, they are becoming isolated from each other both physically and emotionally. It seems there are countless reasons why consumers may feel they never need to leave their homes, with 34% of Brazilian Millennials (aged 19–35) saying they prefer to contact companies/brands online rather than in-store or over the phone. And smart home technology and delivery services make it easier than ever for consumers to feel they have everything they need under their own roof."

Facilitating connections and creating unique spaces where communities can be built is the next stage in cultivating customer loyalty. Brands who position their physical and virtual 'space' as places for consumers to meet while also

eating, shopping or taking part in a leisure activity will lead to a boost in not only engagement, but revenue.

Redefining adulthood

With experiences over material things being a key priority for consumers, companies need to focus on campaigns and opportunities that focus on making life memorable. Taking a technology-first approach could be the answer, as more and more consumers are commonly relying on technology to manage their everyday 'adult' tasks. In fact, a third (33%) of US consumers agree they would rather interact with people online than in person.

Despite more convenience and opportunity, the challenges of adulthood have not disappeared. Those looking to capitalise on this will serve as a resource for these hurdles by making responsibilities feel more manageable and even fun (sometimes). Flexibility is the name of the game. With a growing remote workforce, consumers' daily lives are fluid and brands have to adapt to lifestyles no longer defined by nine to five work cultures.

2 October 2018

*Mintropolitans are broadly defined by Mintel as those who represent a significant, sophisticated consuming group (aged 20–49) who pursue quality of life rather than just wealth, are well educated, and are the potential trendsetters.

What do children in the UK spend their money on?

Children aged 15 years spent more than three times that of a seven-year-old, new data have revealed. Spending data for the financial years 2015 to 2017 show that, on average, 15-year-olds spent £25.00 a week, compared with seven-year-olds, who spent £7.40. Children aged between seven and 15 years were asked to keep a diary of everything they spent their money on within a two-week period, from pocket money, gifts or through a job such as a paper round.

The information collected and published as part of *Family Spending* shows for the first time since 2004 how children behave as consumers.

Age and spending preferences

On average, children aged between seven and 15 years spent £12.40 a week. Broken down into single age years, the amount they spent increased with age.

Expenditure by children by single year of age, UK, financial year ending 2015 to 2017

Average weekly Spend (£)

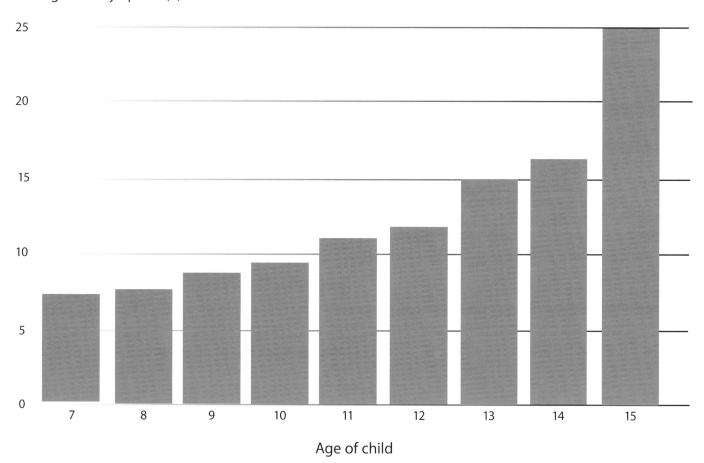

Age of child

Source: *Family spending in the UK*

Top spending categories for children aged 7 to 15 years old, UK, financial year ending 2015 to 2017

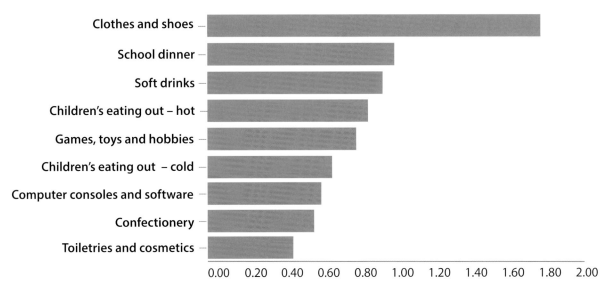

Source: Family spending in the UK

Toiletries and cosmetics separate the sexes

Girls and boys aged seven to 12 years spent broadly similar amounts, but the gap widened as children entered their teenage years, where girls spent an average of £2.80 a week more than boys.

Boys and girls spent differing amounts on different things. One area that separated the sexes was toiletries and cosmetics which includes items such as soap, shampoo and makeup.

Boys of all age ranges spent less than ten pence per week on toiletries and cosmetics, with only 2% buying at least one of these items, compared with 17% of girls.

In contrast, spending on toiletries and cosmetics by girls increased with age; seven to nine-year-old girls spent 20 pence a week, rising to £1.70 for girls aged 13 to 15 years.

Overall children's spending by category

Children spent the most on clothes and shoes, followed by school dinners and soft drinks.

The analysis shows that 56% of seven to 15-year-olds bought at least one soft drink in a two-week period, and mainly drank them away from home.

The older children were, the more likely they were to buy soft drinks; 75% of 13 to 15-year-olds bought at least one soft drink, compared with 58% of ten to 12-year-olds and 38% of seven to nine-year-olds.

The data also show that almost half (48%) of all children spent money on confectionery, which includes chocolate, in a two-week period.

Games, toys and hobbies was the top spending category for seven-to-nine-year-olds, who spent £1.30 a week on average, on items such as jigsaw puzzles, teddy bears and card games.

A quarter of children aged between seven and nine years bought at least one item that fell into this category, compared with 14% of ten to 12-year-olds and 5% of 13 to 15-year-olds.

15 February 2018

Consumer behaviour and retail trends 2018

'Almost all members of Generation Z prefer to shop in bricks-and-mortar stores' – IBM & National Retail Federation.

By Somya Mehta

Online sales continue to grow in importance, as shown by our compilation of ecommerce growth trends. But for many businesses, the days of double-digit, year-on-year growth in online sales are over. We are now in the era of ecommerce optimisation where, to maintain growth, businesses are having to innovate their growth strategy, for making their online experiences engaging and persuasive.

As the world of digital continues to transform, with different generational segments of the population adapting to technology at their own distinct pace, marketers keep a close eye on retail ecommerce trends and developments. With artificial intelligence being a hot topic for the future of marketing, trends like conversational commerce, using chatbots and voice search have been closely associated to widely-adopted online shopping habits amongst Millennials as well as other population segments. More and more stores are moving online and constantly taking measures to improve their online shopping experience and multichannel approach.

Much like the world of digital, consumer shopping behaviour continues to evolve, as consumers discover new opportunities, both online and offline. In fact, a recent retail trends survey, commissioned by a leading London-based international brand experience consultancy, has revealed that almost three-quarters of Millennials still prefer stores to online shopping. Who would have thought? In this world of digital, Millennials, often regarded as an immensely digital-savvy generation, still prefers to shop in a physical store.

The survey was conducted among 2,000 18 to 35-year-olds living in a number of UK cities.

The 2018 Retail Sector report, titled *The Convergence Continuum* looks at how the future of shopping has converged into a 'continuum' of formats, and how consumers, brands and technology are adapting to these changes. Here are the key findings of their research:

- 74% still prefer physical stores compared to just 26% preferring online shopping, with 36% preferring shopping malls.

- 80% of people went shopping as a day trip in the last month, with 50% of those going in the last week.

- 51% would love to navigate, get information and pay using their phone in-store, which is an example of omnichannel retail.

- 46% think staff hinder the shopping experience, but 48% still value help.

- 70% prefer staff but maybe just at the pay point, while 28% would happily shop without staff.

- 71% want store staff to be more knowledgeable.

- 45% would revisit stores that offered workshops and tutorials, while 23% just want to shop.

- 77% of people are open to the idea of handing over data in exchange for discounts.

- 56% would like their click and collect point to offer them a space to try on clothes and facilitate their returns and refunds.

- 73% of people prefer home delivery over click and collect.

- 49% say the most loved element of the in-store experience is touching and trying things out.

- 69% of store card holders believe they are valuable and encourage them to shop at the same store.

Commenting on the report, I-AM Group Partner, Pete Champion, said: 'Both online and offline, people prefer multi-brand stores over mono-brand ones. Retail has undergone a seismic change in the last decade. Though this has been largely driven by technology, our consumer attitudes to what shopping is and does has shifted dramatically and our needs, platforms and spaces have converged. We no longer shop in specific bursts, rather shopping hums along at our pace of life.

'Retail has become a continuous chain-reaction of movements, events, experiences and motives. Shopping has become relative – relative to context, person and place and has moulded into four dimensions of space and time. Shopping is no longer about the what and where, but how and when.'

In today's fast-paced, technology-oriented world, consumers are overwhelmed with content. Be it through ads, offers, emails, texts, social media and everything else, the industry has reached a point of 'content shock where consumers cannot consume much more content than they already are.' Hence, the way brands devise their digital marketing strategy, to capture their audience's attention, needs to change. Brands need to focus on the micro-moments of their customers' behaviours.'

Think with Google outlines micro-moments marketing as, 'What used to be our predictable, daily sessions online have been replaced by many fragmented interactions that now occur instantaneously. There are hundreds of these moments everyday – checking the time, texting a spouse, chatting with friends on social media. But then there are the other moments – the I-want-to-know moments, I-want-to-go moments, I-want-to-do moments and I-want-to-buy moments – that really matter. We call these micro-moments, and they're game changers for both consumers and brands.'

5 July 2018

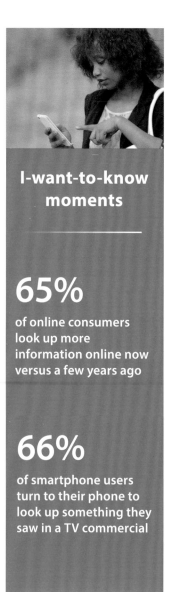

I-want-to-know moments

65%
of online consumers look up more information online now versus a few years ago

66%
of smartphone users turn to their phone to look up something they saw in a TV commercial

I-want-to-go moments

2X
increase in 'near me' search interest in the past year

82%
of smartphone users use a search engine when looking for a local business

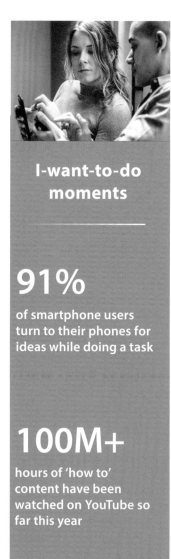

I-want-to-do moments

91%
of smartphone users turn to their phones for ideas while doing a task

100M+
hours of 'how to' content have been watched on YouTube so far this year

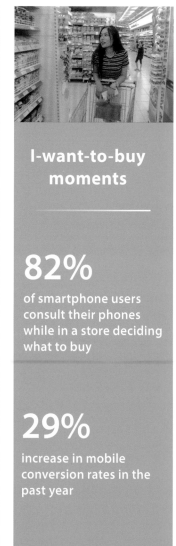

I-want-to-buy moments

82%
of smartphone users consult their phones while in a store deciding what to buy

29%
increase in mobile conversion rates in the past year

Adapted from Smart Insights

Research shows most online consumer contracts are incomprehensible, but still legally binding

An article from **The Conversation.**

By Samuel Becher, Associate Professor of Business Law, Victoria University of Wellington

THE CONVERSATION

Most of us will have entered into consumer contracts with large companies and ticked a box to confirm we understand the terms and conditions – without bothering to read the fine print.

We accept standard form contracts when using social media, booking flights, opening a bank account, subscribing to a gym or renting a car. In all these cases, companies offer predrafted standardised agreements that are not negotiable.

At the same time, consumers are legally assumed to read the terms and conditions of their contracts. Because of this 'duty to read', consumers are held responsible for the written terms of their agreements, regardless of whether they read them or not.

While consumers have the legal burden to read their contracts,

companies do not have a general duty to offer readable ones. As our research shows, most of them are incomprehensible.

Checking readability

We have studied popular online consumer contracts and examined the readability of the 500 most popular sign-in-wrap contracts in the United States.

These contracts, now used routinely by popular companies such as Facebook, Amazon, Uber and Airbnb, assume that the user agrees to the website's terms and conditions by signing up. During the sign-up process, the website provides a hyperlink to its terms and conditions. But the consumer is not required to actually access the terms.

Many scholars argue that consumers do not read their contracts. Nonetheless, courts enforce these contracts based on the assumption that consumers had an opportunity to read them. In other words, according to this reasoning, consumers freely choose to ignore these contracts.

To examine this legal argument, we applied two well-established linguistic tools to check if consumers can actually read sign-in-wrap contracts. We used the Flesch Reading Ease and the Flesch-Kincaid tests. Both tests are based on two factors: the average sentence length and the average number of syllables per word.

Consumer contracts as dense as academic papers

We found that according to these criteria, the contracts examined in our sample are very hard to read. In fact, they are written at the same level as academic articles. Reading these agreements requires, on average, more than 14 years of education. This result is troubling, given the recommended reading level for consumer materials is eighth grade.

Our study shows consumers cannot be expected to read their contracts. A contract is based on mutual assent, but consumers cannot truly assent to something they cannot read.

We hope such findings will encourage policymakers to revisit their approach to consumer contracts. For starters, legislatures should require companies to better communicate their terms. Beyond that, we should also detail systematic and objective criteria as to what is readable.

At the same time, courts should not assume consumers can read their contracts. Judges should hence be more willing to excuse consumers from unreadable agreements.

Where to from here?

Linguistic tests may serve as a good starting point. But such tools should be used only as a perquisite legal standard for examining readability. Companies might deliberately generate good readability scores but that does not necessarily mean the text is actually easy to understand.

The purpose of plain language requirements is not to increase readability per se. Rather, it is to improve the chances that users will be able to understand these agreements, shop among them, and make informed decisions.

Making contracts readable does not rest other concerns, such as the incorporation of unfair terms. Policymakers need to take further steps to level the consumer-business playing field. Currently, the law neglects to impose on companies a clear and operational duty to draft readable contracts. Without a clear incentive, companies will continue to use unreadable texts as their contracts.

This research is a joint project, co-authored with Dr Uri Benoliel at the College of Law and Business in Ramat Gan, Israel.

Rethinking consumerism for the sake of young people's mental health (and the planet)

Rethinking consumerism will not only boost environmental protection – it will also help to tackle the crisis in young people's mental health.

Blogpost by Chris Large, Global Action Plan – Our Lives. Our Planet.

What if the solution to the mental health crisis facing young people is the same as tackling environmental degradation? That solution is at hand – moving beyond consumerism.

The environmental damage of consuming resources at the current rate is well known. Across the world, 60% more resources are consumed every year than the sustainable rate, driving the pollution, climate change and ecosystem damage that are documented in ever more distressing detail.

Evidence about the effects of consumerism on mental health and wellbeing is also building, and it makes similarly painful reading. And yet consumerism remains one of society's few unquestioned doctrines. We're prepared to have lengthy debates about many complex issues, from EU membership to wearing religious symbols at work. But whether society should keep consuming at a rate which destroys the natural environment while damaging young people's mental health is perhaps just too challenging a topic to confront.

Maybe this is why projects to move society beyond consumerism receive the least funding from environment sector grant makers.

When faced with an economic downturn, politicians tell people to go out and spend on the high street as though their lives depended on it. The opposite is true. Society is dependent on a healthy environment, and it transpires that personal wellbeing is also boosted by breaking away from the consumerist pressure to buy, buy, buy.

Consumption and wellbeing

Social scientists have known for years that young people whose 'operating system' aims to accumulate ever more stuff (trainers, houses, jewellery, cars, bags, mobile phones) are less happy than those who prioritise heartier pursuits.

The traits of teens reporting higher wellbeing include spending time with friends and family, hobbies that expand the mind, finding a purpose inside or outside of work, exercising more, spending more time outdoors, and active community involvement.

Buying stuff to meet our needs of course plays an important role in people's lives, but wellbeing studies illustrate that materialistic tendencies are linked to decreased life satisfaction, happiness, vitality and social cooperation, and increases in depression, anxiety, racism and antisocial behaviour.

With young people exposed to more advertising than ever before, including through social media, where their friends and others they follow might be being paid to promote that new jacket they're wearing, shouldn't we be discussing and debating the impacts of consumerism on wellbeing?

According to the Varkey Foundation, British Millennials have the second worst mental wellbeing in the world, second only to Japan. Depression rates have doubled in a decade with as many as 24% of girls and 9% of boys aged 14 in the UK experiencing symptoms of depression. One in four young women between the ages of 16 and 24 report having self-harmed and 93% of teachers report increased levels of mental illness in children and young people. Is consumerism partly to blame?

Materialism and self-esteem

Consumerism thrives on the importance of appearance, as promoted by adverts, music videos and social media. Alongside wellbeing experts, I find it hard to imagine that this influence does not contribute to the mental health crisis. Charity Young Minds explains that:

'Social media puts pressure on girls to live their lives in the public domain, to present a personal "brand" from a young age, and to seek reassurance in the form of likes and shares.' A Girl Guides survey found that 42% of 11–16-year-olds are "ashamed about the way they look" (most of the time or often) and the percentage of girls and young women aged seven to 21 saying they are "happy with how they look" dropped from 73% to only 61% over five years.

UNICEF reports that those from low-income families may be particularly vulnerable to marketing efforts, with poorer 11–17-year-olds being more materialistic than their wealthier counterparts, which appears to be associated with lower self-esteem among impoverished teens.

The long shadow of consumerism

Children living in the UK's consumerist society are by no means the only children affected by the system that drives demand for goods. Consumerism casts a dark shadow on young people's lives on the other side of the planet. For example, an estimated 20,000 children work in mines retrieving mica, the mineral that adds an iridescent shimmer to some eyeshadows and blushers.

I believe that this upsetting situation, at home and abroad, requires urgent action, and there is a major cause for hope among this bleak picture. The hope springs from the strength and simplicity of the post-consumerist destination. A life where young people experience less pressure to buy stuff and look good, and feel free to spend more time doing things that really make them happy, is also a life that preserves the ecosystems that underpin a prosperous society.

A bright post-consumerist future

To reach a post-consumerist society, the environment sector could lead by transforming the conversation about consumption. The real value to society lies in consuming less physical things, not just handling waste better or building the circular economy. It's hard to envisage a sure-fire scenario for planetary sustainability in which the current level of consumption of physical goods is maintained, no matter what level of renewable energy and material recycling exists. That is before factoring in the increased consumption of materials by the growing middle-class of economically growing countries such as India and China.

The good news is that the studies of materialistic lifestyles show that people who rely less on physical materials for happiness (after base needs are met) are generally happier. Consuming less stuff isn't about going backwards, or making a sacrifice – an accusation often levelled at the environment sector. Consuming less is about focusing on what really makes young people happy. When it comes to consumption levels in a wealthy society, it appears that less is really more.

24 May 2018

SHE'S AWESOME! I'D DIE TO LOOK LIKE HER.

YOU'RE KIDDING? THAT'S NOT REAL. IT'S BEEN PHOTOSHOPPED, ENHANCED, AIRBRUSHED, HIGHLIGHTED AND WITH AN OBVIOUS FAKE BACKGROUND IT'S ALL FAKE!

The above information is reprinted with kind permission from Chris Large and Environmental Funders Network.
© EFN2019

www.greenfunders.org
www.globalactionplan.org.uk

Black Friday 2018 UK

In the UK, Black Friday is by far the biggest shopping event of the year. It always falls on the Friday after Thanksgiving in the USA.

Black Friday in the United Kingdom

This event, known previously only in the States, has gained a truly worldwide popularity within just a few years. In the United Kingdom – 95% of respondents know what Black Friday is.

Black Friday Global's analysis team has been closely following this trend for the past several years. We know exactly how relevant this event is for retailers, the domestic and local economy, as well as for average consumers.

How is the interest in shopping and discounts growing among the British in November? Which categories of goods are characterised by the highest demand? How much money do the British spend during the Black Friday shopping craze and how are they different from the other nations? We've analysed Black Friday statistics and conducted surveys in 55 countries to answer the above questions. Here are the results of our analysis.

Global recognition

Black Friday is now a phenomenon for a reason. Google's data suggests that in the last five years the interest of internet users in this event has more than doubled. Every year, in almost every country, the shopping fever results in new sales records. Only in Western Hemisphere countries, where trends from the US appear faster, a moderate increase in Black Friday discounts is noted.

Over the past five years, the popularity of this shopping event has been growing consistently. The survey suggests that three out of five British will participate in Black Friday this year (an increase of one percentage point compared to 2017). The majority of consumers will shop both online and offline (64%), the rest will either opt for traditional offline-only (12%) or online-only (24%) options. For comparison, in 2017 the percentage of users choosing brick and mortar stores only was higher by almost a half (from 11.9% to 23.6%).

Boosting the global economy

Such a great Black Friday recognition results in sales number surges each year. In each of the 55 analysed countries, the number of online transactions on Black Friday increased significantly when compared to the regular day. Take Greece for example, where users have made 2,600% more purchases than usual or South Africa with 2,571% growth in transaction number. However, in no other country was Black Friday interest as big as in Pakistan, where users activity was higher by enormous 11,525%.

Unsurprisingly so, November is usually the month where most profits are generated. According to certain estimates, around 20% of annual turnover is being made in November.

What's more, our internal data allows us to re-evaluate that in certain markets – e.g. the UK, Greece, RSA – where even every third transaction is taking place in November.

Hard money

The results of the survey show that users in North America and Europe are willing to spend the most during Black Friday. On the contrary, Asian customers – i.e. in Pakistan, Malaysia, Philippines – are planning to spend relatively small amounts of money. The average British bargain hunter is willing to pay £300 ($400) in total for his/her Black Friday shopping cart. That is almost $115 less than American consumers, and almost $89 less than Canadians.

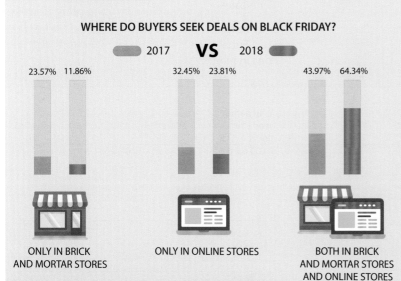

BLACK FRIDAY IN THE UK

Bargain hunters in the UK

63.01% participated in 2017

64.12% participated in 2018

95% of Brits know what Black Friday is

WHERE DO BUYERS SEEK DEALS ON BLACK FRIDAY?

2017 VS 2018

ONLY IN BRICK AND MORTAR STORES: 23.57% 11.86%

ONLY IN ONLINE STORES: 32.45% 23.81%

BOTH IN BRICK AND MORTAR STORES AND ONLINE STORES: 43.97% 64.34%

WHICH PRODUCTS ARE THE MOST POPULAR ON BLACK FRIDAY?

10. Underwear

 1. Clothes

9. Sports accessories

 2. Electronics

8. Books

 3. Shoes

7. Children's products

 4. Cosmetics & perfumes

 6. Gifts

 5. Home appliances

Pieces of Black Friday cake

Every year, the world press feeds us with dozens of photos of crowds besieging electronics stores. Surprisingly though, the results of our survey state that clothes, not electronics, are the actual apple of bargain hunters' eyes. Consumer electronics category came second in our ranking. On the other side of the scale, books, sports accessories and underwear were the least popular items to buy.

Unusual markdowns

Black Friday is well known for its discounts reaching as high as 80–90%. Even though the number of items available for a single dollar or with 90% discount is highly limited, those participating in Black Friday can count on legitimate bargains. According to our Black Friday 2017 data, the biggest discounts were available for Americans (68% average markdown), Canadians (66%) and Ukrainians (66%). A little less impressive rebates were found in Russia (58% average markdown), Brazil (57%) and Turkey (56%). World's average sets around 55% off.

As the average discount in the UK online stores reached 62% last year, when forecasting British Black Friday 2018 expenses, it could translate into £489 of possible average savings.

Black Friday figures in the United Kingdom

- 95% of British know what Black Friday is, and 64% are willing to participate in the shopping spree this year

- 64% of bargain hunters will choose both online and offline sales

- An average British person will spend £300 during Black Friday sales, with clothes, electronics and shoes in mind

November 2018

Methodology and data sources: This report was created based on data provided by Picodi.com – a global discounts provider existing since 2010. Black-Friday.Global – dedicated to Black Friday deals – was created by Picodi.com. 12,000 participants from 55 countries took part in the survey.

www.black-friday.global

Black Friday vs Cyber Monday: which is bigger?

Black Friday vs Cyber Monday. Both events are considered to be one of the biggest retail days of the year, with a number of shoppers using them to start on their Christmas shopping early and save on the best deals. With only two days between the events, which one of them is bigger?

By Pamela Kokoszka

Black Friday

Black Friday is an informal name for the day following Thanksgiving day in the US, which has been regarded as the beginning of the country's Christmas shopping since 1952.

According to market research company Ipsos, Black Friday has been the busiest shopping day of the year in the US since 2005. In 2014, spending on Black Friday fell for the first time since the 2008 recession.

Since the start of the 21st century, retailers with origins in the US have attempted to introduce Black Friday in the UK. While at the beginning the event was not very popular among both retailers and shoppers, it has quickly picked up and according to UK's online retail association IMRG, the amount spent on UK online retail sites on Black Friday in 2017 totalled £1.39 billion.

Meanwhile, based on data from Adobe Analytics, a record $5.03 billion was spent online on Black Friday in the US.

According to Adobe Analytics, this year Black Friday is expected to generate $5.8 billion in online sales in the US,

an increase of 15.3% on 2017. Shoppers are expected to spend $2.44 billion on mobile devices alone.

During the Black Friday weekend that also includes Thanksgiving, the number of shoppers in the US, both in store and online has reached 174 million. This year this number is expected to reach 180 million according to the National Retail Federation.

The National Retail Federation has also found that the average spend per shopper in the US was £335.47 in 2017, with that number expected to grow to $340.33 this year.

Meanwhile, according to a survey by Salmon, a Wunderman Commerce company, Black Friday sales in the UK are expected to reach £4.75 billion.

Cyber Monday

Cyber Monday was introduced in the US in 2005 by the marketing team at Shop.org, a division of the National Retail Federation, and takes place on the Monday after Black Friday. The idea behind Cyber Monday was to provide online retailers with an alternative to Black Friday, which typically takes places in the store. As at the time of Cyber Monday's inception, most shoppers were still shopping at brick-and-mortar retailers, there was a need to persuade customers to shop online.

Cyber Monday has not just caught on in the US, but also in the UK, Canada, France, Portugal and New Zealand, among other nations. ComScore reported that online spending in the US on Cyber Monday increased 25% to $608 million in 2006, 21% to $733 million in 2007 and 15% to $846 million in 2008. In 2010, Cyber Monday sales reached $1 billion mark for the first time. ComScore also added that in 2010 Cyber Monday was the busiest online shopping day of the year.

Since today most shopping is done online, Cyber Monday is growing in strength both in the US and the UK, becoming one of the most important shopping days of the year with new record number of sales each year.

Adobe Analytics reported a record $6.59 billion was spent online on Cyber Monday in the US in 2017, nearly doubling the total sales of $3.45 billion from 2016.

This year, US shoppers are expected to spend $7.25 billion according to a research by Adobe Analytics, with $2.5 billion expected to be spent on online shopping on mobile devices.

In addition, 95 million shoppers in the US are expected to take part in Cyber Monday sales, in comparison to 81 million from the year before.

Verdict: Black Friday vs Cyber Monday, which one is bigger?

In 2017, Black Friday was the most popular in-store shopping event, cited by 77 million consumers according to the US National Retail Federations.

However, Cyber Monday was the most popular online shopping event with 81 million shoppers, compared to 66 million online shoppers on Black Friday.

In terms of online sales in 2017, Cyber Monday overtook Black Friday by $1.56 billion. While in terms of predictions for 2018, Cyber Monday is expected to generate $1.45 billion more than Black Friday in the US this year.

According to the findings above, Cyber Monday has overtaken Black Friday as the biggest US shopping event during the Thanksgiving weekend.

22 November 2018

Cadbury chocolate Easter eggs to get smaller in latest example of food 'shrinkflation'

By Florence Snead

In brief

- Some eggs will suffer a 7% size reduction
- Prices are going down by 2.5%

With its vast array of all things chocolate, Easter is a tempting time of year for those of us bestowed with a sweet tooth.

But shoppers looking to indulge in some egg-shaped goodies may find their money stretches less far this year after it emerged a major retailer's Easter eggs would be getting smaller.

In the latest example of 'shrinkflation', Cadbury confirmed a number of its eggs were set to shrink in size but to a greater extent than their prices.

Shrinking in size

According to the trade magazine *The Grocer*, the chocolate giant's Crunchie and large Creme Eggs will both come down from 278g to 258g, a reduction of around 7%.

Meanwhile its Heroes egg will go from 274g to 254g, Twirl from 282g to 262g and the Double Decker from 307g to 287g.

But their recommended retail prices (RRP) will only go down 2.5 per cent from £6.15 to £6, it added.

It marks the latest in a string of shrinking products and comes just weeks after the Office for National Statistics (ONS) claimed 206 items got smaller between September 2015 and June 2017.

Of those that shrank, its analysis found the majority were food and drink products.

Alex Neill, managing director of home products and servicers at the consumer group *Which?*, said there had been a trend in recent years for items getting smaller while staying the same price.

'Taken together, these practices can have a real impact at a time when many households are already facing a squeeze on their finances,' she said.

'Manufacturers and retailers may have legitimate reasons to make changes to the size of their products, but they must be upfront with their customers so that people can make an informed choice about how to spend their money.'

'Retailers free to set their own prices'

A spokesman for Cadbury said they 'always try where possible to reduce the RRP when we need to make a reduction to the size or weight of our products'.

'Like all food manufacturers, we sometimes have to make changes to ensure that people can continue to buy their favourite Easter treats at affordable prices,' they said.

'We've worked hard to ensure we're still offering families great value for money across what we believe will be a popular product this Easter and as always, retailers are free to set their own prices.'

But shoppers on the lookout for an Easter treat need not necessarily resign themselves to having to fork out more, according to MoneySavingExpert deputy editor Guy Anker.

'If you are buying [chocolate] you will often find it is smaller than they were but if you look carefully there will be deals,' he told *i*.

'Savvy shoppers can beat shrinkflation by looking out for the bargains which often exist at the supermarkets and other smaller stores that sell chocolate.'

Rising costs

According to the Food and Drink Federation, there have been 'sharp increases' in the cost of essential ingredients, packaging and other raw materials used to make food and drink products in recent years.

'The falling strength of the pound has added to these massive cost pressures,' they added.

'This is in addition to the huge costs many manufacturers are incurring as they prepare for a potential no deal Brexit scenario.

'The majority of food and drink companies have taken a hit on already tight margins in the notoriously competitive UK grocery market.

'Some companies have reached a point where to protect jobs they must either seek to share a modest price increase with retailers or reduce portion sizes.

'The decision on which of these options to pursue is informed by UK supermarkets who ultimately set the prices faced by consumers and have buyer power over which products are placed on their shelves.'

8 February 2019

Shrinkflation: for those struggling, it's about more than just chocolate bars

By Frances Ryan

I f late capitalism can be boiled down to a social media-friendly phrase, look no further than 'shrinkflation' – when goods are made smaller but still sold at exactly the same price. Figures from the Office for National Statistics reveal that as many as 206 products were made smaller between September 2015 and June 2017.

High-profile examples include Mars shrinking Maltesers, M&Ms and Minstrels by up to 15%, while Birds Eye cut the number of fish fingers in a packet from 12 to 10. The makers of Toblerone sent the internet into frenzy in 2016 after it widened the gap between the distinctive triangular chunks.

Last year, after the backlash, it reverted the bar to its original shape – but bigger, and with a higher price.

The reasons behind the trend are understandable; retailers blame rising costs and increasing competition on the high street, as well as the Brexit-linked fall in the pound. The problem is, it feels sneaky – corporations quietly giving their so-called valued customers less, while taking the same money, and hoping no one will notice. Or worse, knowing we will and betting we'll buy it anyway.

Add it all up and shrinkage isn't just an annoyance. For the millions of people struggling with food insecurity, it's the difference between being able to afford the weekly shop or not. Chocolates make the headlines, but this trend largely affects everyday essentials. The ONS found most

size changes occur with household items such as toilet rolls, nappies and washing-up liquid, while foods with the highest numbers of product size changes included bread and meat.

No matter what businesses are up against, shrinkflation sums up multimillion-pound companies choosing to push the cost on to already squeezed families. That leaves a bad taste in the mouth.

22 January 2019

Social media has made schoolchildren more fashion conscious than ever – and parents are footing the bill

An article from **The Conversation.**

THE CONVERSATION

By Emily Moorlock, Senior Lecturer in Marketing, Sheffield Hallam University

New pencil cases, shoes, bags and coats might line the classrooms, but for many parents, the additional financial strain associated with sending their teenagers back to school can be significant.

According to reports by The Children's Society, families with children at secondary school pay, on average, more than £300 per child every year in school uniform costs. A 2015 government report found a fifth of low-income parents have suffered financial hardship from having to purchase school uniforms. This figure was lower where parents were able to purchase the uniform from anywhere (such as supermarkets) – rather than specific school uniform shops.

But most schools require pupils to wear a uniform branded with the school emblem rather than generic pieces – and this can further increase the cost. This is despite the Government pledging to lower school uniform costs.

The right brands

But additional school paraphernalia is not as strictly controlled by schools or the Government. And many teenagers want a long list of branded items – from shoes, bags and mobile phones to the crisps in their lunchbox.

Consumerism is entering the playground and placing further pressure on already stretched parents. Research shows consumerism is an intrinsic part of human nature. And many teenagers perceive possessions as symbols of their identity – making judgements about their peers based on the brands they choose.

The same research has also shown that consumerism acts as a coping mechanism in situations where an individual experiences feelings of anxiety, uncertainty and insecurity.

The teenage years are rife with physical and emotional changes, which amplify these feelings. And brands can allow teenagers to forge their identity at a turbulent time when they are transitioning into adulthood and establishing who they are.

Material happiness

Some teenagers associate consuming the 'right' brands with achieving happiness and peer approval. But research shows that consumerism negatively correlates to overall life satisfaction. In this way, then, the need for constant peer comparison and approval can negatively impact teenager well-being – particularly self-esteem. It has been suggested that a societal shift among younger generations towards extrinsic goals – which relate to the need to acquire material possessions and peer acceptance over intrinsic goals that link to personal development and self-acceptance – have led to an increase in consumerism.

This creates a situation where teenagers place greater emphasis on money, possessions and status over personal growth and relationships. As well as pressure for teenagers to consume and gain peer acceptance. This has been linked to the rise in teenager anxiety, particularly among girls.

Vicious cycle

My research finds members of younger generations struggle to escape consumerism.

Many feel an inherent need to consume the 'right' brands to gain a sense of belonging to a particular peer group. The 'right' brand is considered to be a brand that allows the teenager to portray a desirable image of who they are or who they aspire to be to the world.

Many adults I spoke to as part of my research even vividly recalled instances in their teenage years when they had been bullied at school for being associated with the wrong brand. This included having a brand of mobile phone their peers considered to be cheap, and wearing unbranded trainers for PE. These experiences led to a greater emphasis being placed on certain brands in the transition from teenager to adult to avoid negative feelings associated with the 'wrong' brand.

Teenagers make judgements about their peers based on the brands they choose.

Social media can also exacerbate this need to consume and have the 'right' brands – with many peers and online influencers posting glossier versions (or even complete fabrications) of reality. Social media also allows for constant social comparison. This can increase the need for teenagers to keep up with their peers to avoid scrutiny – which creates a vicious cycle. This makes it difficult for teenagers to step back and differentiate the idealised self-image their peers portray online from reality, and so they feel pressure to follow suit.

School pressures

In the UK, more than 4 million children live in poverty. And research shows the impact of consumerism on teenagers is greater for those from lower-income families.

These teenagers can be more susceptible to peer influence. They may use brands to emulate an image of a richer counterpart to avoid being teased for being poor. This helps them to achieve and maintain social acceptance, while reducing feelings of personal inadequacy and anxiety.

It's clear that at school having a particular brand can mean the difference between popularity and rejection. To tackle this, the Government should look to place a cap on the amount schools are able to charge for branded uniforms. Schools could also help by ensuring items such as school bags and shoes are generic and unbranded to help reduce some of the pressure on parents and teenagers alike.

5 September 2018

Consumer rights

If you buy something from a shop and you are not happy with it you have certain rights. You have the right to get a full refund, repair or replacement if what you bought isn't:

- of a satisfactory quality – it should not be faulty or damaged
- fit for purpose – it should be able to do the task you bought it for
- as described – it must match the description given to you when you bought it.

Within 30 days

You have a legal right to get a refund from a retailer, as long as you do it within 30 days. The refund period can sometimes be longer than 30 days but this depends on the shop.

Your right to return goods lies with the retailer, not the manufacturer. For example, if you buy a microwave and it breaks down a week later you can get a refund or replacement.

You can get this refund or replacement from the shop that sold the microwave to you. Not the company that made the microwave.

After 30 days

If the 30-day refund period has passed, you may still be able to get a refund if your item is faulty.

But before you can ask for a refund, you must give the shop a chance to either repair or replace your item.

You can choose whether to have your item repaired or replaced. But the shop can refuse your choice if the other option is cheaper.

Faulty items

If you find a fault with something within six months of buying it, it's assumed the fault was there when you bought it. The shop must fix it, replace it or give you a full refund.

If you find the fault more than six months after you bought it, you have to prove it was faulty when you got it. Otherwise the shop doesn't have to give you a refund.

If the goods do not last a reasonable length of time (up to five years) you may be entitled to some money back.

Returning goods bought during a sale

You have the same right to get a return or refund if you bought something during a sale. But only if it's faulty.

If you ask for a refund on a sale item, your refund will be the price you paid for it.

This will be the case even if the sale has ended and it's returned to its original price.

Example

You buy something for £20 during a sale but then its price goes back up to £50 when the sale ends.

If you want to return the item and get a refund, the most you can get is £20.

You can only return non-faulty goods bought in-store, for a refund or exchange, if the store has a returns policy.

Shops don't have to have a returns policy for purchases made in store. But if they do, they must stick to it. Your statutory rights (Consumer Rights Act 2015) still apply.

Shops often put restrictions on returning sale items, so check the returns policy before you buy. Most retailers put time limits for returning non-faulty goods, e.g. 28 days.

Ordered goods that arrive late

If you order something and have it delivered to your home, it usually has to be delivered not more than 30 days after you bought it. Unless you've been told it'll be delivered by a different date.

You could have the right to cancel and get a full refund if the shop hasn't delivered:

- within 30 days
- on another date you've agreed to.

But this is only if:

- the delivery is later than agreed and you needed it on time, or
- you did not need it on time but you can't agree on another reasonable delivery date.

Retailers are responsible for goods until they reach you. If they use a delivery company and the delivery is late, the retailer can't use this as an excuse. They must arrange a refund.

Challenging terms and conditions

When you buy something, you're entering into a contract with the shop you buy it from.

The shop can use whatever terms and conditions they want in this contract, but they have to be fair.

A contract term can be checked for fairness if it is not transparent (explained in language that's easy to understand), and prominent (brought to the customer's attention).

You have the right to challenge part of a contract if you don't think it's fair. This may include:

- extra fees and charges hidden in the small print
- something that tries to restrict your legal rights
- charging you a lot of money to cancel a contract

- a term that lets them change the product you ordered
- raising the price before your order is shipped out.

If you think a contract term is unfair, complain to the trader you bought it from.

If they don't agree, get legal advice before breaking the terms of the contract. For example by cancelling a purchase after the required period.

As a last resort, you could take the trader to court and the court will decide whether a term is unfair.

If the court decides that a term is unfair, you may be able to ignore the term or even cancel your contract without having to pay a cancellation fee.

Buying digital products

The above rights are based on physical items you can buy from a shop or have delivered to your house.

Your rights are different when dealing with digital products, such as:

- games
- movies
- music
- apps.

If you download something you do not have a legal right to get a refund. But you do have the right to make sure your download works.

If your digital content does not meet these criteria and develops a fault, you have the right to have it repaired or replaced.

You can ask the retailer to repair or replace a download if it:

- doesn't play right
- is faulty in any other way.

If it's not possible to repair or replace your download, you can get a price reduction of up to 100% of the cost.

A retailer has to give you compensation if a download causes damage to your:

- computer
- smartphone
- tablet
- software.

4 June 2018

National Consumer Week 2018

We're supporting National Consumer Week, which aims to champion consumer rights in areas where there is risk of consumers being treated unfairly. This year, the area we're focusing on is online marketplaces – specifically, the selling of goods.

National Consumer Week is a joint awareness campaign by the Consumer Protection Partnership – of which the ASA is a member – a group of bodies whose aim is to tackle misleading practices that can lead to consumer harm.

Most of us now interact with the world online, whether that's purchasing goods or services or accessing entertainment or information. It's crucial, therefore, that the right protections exist to make sure we're doing so in safety.

Our recently launched five-year strategy aims to do more to protect consumers online, through steps we've already taken and our ambitions for the next five years. We want to bust myths such as online advertising being a 'wild west' – the UK Advertising Codes apply as equally online as they do in broadcast or print media.

With online shopping commonplace and for many, replacing more traditional shopping entirely due to convenience and flexibility, it is vital to be able to shop safely online. Recent polling indicates three-quarters (76%) of UK adults now use online marketplaces.

According to Citizens Advice, more than 13,000 problems with purchases on online marketplaces were reported last year. Calls about problems with purchases in these forums have increased by 35% over the past four years.

One of the main consumer issues was 'goods being misdescribed in the sales adverts', in 13% of cases. Research also shows over 50% of customers aren't aware that they have fewer rights when they buy from a private seller, compared to if they buy from a business.

One complaint to the ASA can be enough to trigger an investigation and potentially result in an upheld ruling.

We've put together some facts and figures about the kinds of issues we see consumers facing when using online marketplaces.

Overall, we receive around 30,000 complaints a year. In 2018 so far, we have received over 700 complaints relating to 365 ads in connection with online marketplaces. The majority of complaints didn't merit investigation, and of those that did, most were resolved informally, which means that the advertiser was willing to make immediate changes to resolve the issue quickly and effectively, without a full investigation.

Of these complaints, ten were investigated resulting in six upheld rulings dealing with a range of issues.

Guy Parker, Chief Executive of the ASA, said: 'Online shopping can be great for convenience and good deals, but it's important that people are treated just as fairly online as they are off. We're making sure the same rules apply, and are followed, across all online platforms.'

So, what should you keep an eye out for when browsing online? Below are some to bear in mind to avoid future online shopping strife:

Check the product details carefully

This should include: photos; a description; cost of the item; delivery charges; contact details for the seller (trader or private seller); and any cancellation rights.

Take screenshots of the item you want to buy

This will come in handy if the item you receive is different to what you saw on the website.

Use a payment method that protects you

You'll have a better chance of getting your money back if there's a problem by using a card or PayPal, particularly if it's an overseas seller. Avoid paying by bank transfer.

Go back to the seller if there's a problem

Explain what's happened, how you'd like them to fix it and give a deadline for them to respond. If they don't sort it out, see if there's an alternative dispute resolution service that can help. Report them and the online marketplace to Trading Standards if you think the issue is unfair.

Watch out for VAT-exclusive prices or unclear fees and charges

There shouldn't be any hidden fees – buyers shouldn't discover unexpected surcharges at the end of the shopping experience.

Check where the advertiser is based

Depending on where the product is coming from, delivery times could be affected and it could take longer than you anticipated for the product to arrive.

Be wary of 'was' prices or RRP comparisons and make sure you look at the small print.

Price comparisons that differ significantly from the price at which the product is generally sold are likely to mislead.

And make sure...

...you know your rights. If you see a problem promotion or misleading ad, let us know.

The GDPR: consumer rights for your personal data

By Julia Van Grieken

You're probably aware of 'consumer rights': they are the rules organisations need to follow to stop customers from being exploited. The specifics vary between laws, but they almost always include the rights to remain safe, informed and to lodge complaints.

Though essential, these rights don't reflect the way consumer culture has evolved in recent years. Goods and services are now often exchanged for individuals' personal data, so similar rules are needed for the way that information is processed.

That's where the EU General Data Protection Regulation (GDPR) comes in. A lot has been written about the Regulation's extensive requirements and the potential for massive fines for data breaches, but it's all to create an environment in which individuals can share their information without having to worry about how secure it is.

Data subjects' rights

The GDPR provides individuals with eight rights:

1. **The right to be informed:** Organisations need to tell individuals what data is being collected, how it's being used, how long it will be kept and whether it will be shared with any third parties. This information must be communicated concisely and in plain language.

2. **The right to access:** Individuals can submit subject access requests, which oblige organisations to provide a copy of any personal data concerning the individual. Organisations have one month to produce this information, although there are exceptions for requests that are manifestly unfounded, repetitive or excessive.

3. **The right to rectification:** If the individual discovers that the information an organisation holds on them is inaccurate or incomplete, they can request that it be updated. As with the right to access, organisations have one month to do this, and the same exceptions apply.

4. **The right to erasure** (also known as 'the right to be forgotten'): Individuals can request that organisations erase their data in certain circumstances, such as when the data is no longer necessary, the data was unlawfully processed or it no longer meets the lawful ground for which it was collected. This includes instances where the individual withdraws consent.

5. **The right to restrict processing**: Individuals can request that organisations limit the way an organisation uses personal data. It's an alternative to requesting the erasure of data, and might be used when the individual contests the accuracy of their personal data or when the individual no longer needs the information but the organisation requires it to establish, exercise or defend a legal claim.

6. **The right to data portability:** Individuals are permitted to obtain and reuse their personal data for their own purposes across different services. This right only applies to personal data that an individual has provided to data controllers by way of a contract or consent.

7. **The right to object:** Individuals can object to the processing of personal data that is collected on the grounds of legitimate interests or the performance of a task in the interest/exercise of official authority. Organisations must stop processing information unless they can demonstrate compelling legitimate grounds for the processing that overrides the interests, rights and freedoms of the individual or if the processing is for the establishment or exercise of defence of legal claims.

8. **Rights related to automated decision making including profiling:** The GDPR includes provisions for decisions made with no human involvement, such as profiling, which uses personal data to make calculated assumptions about individuals. There are strict rules about this kind of processing, and individuals are permitted to challenge and request a review of the processing if they believe the rules aren't being followed.

11 April 2018

Holidaymakers benefit from sweeping new consumer rights

'If it looks like a package holiday, with flights and accommodation included in a single transaction, then it should have all the prodigious consumer protection that comes with a proper package.'

By Simon Calder

Major online travel agents appear to be complying with new rules that are designed to provide millions of holidaymakers with far more consumer rights.

The new Package Travel Regulations, which came into force at midnight, comprise the biggest shake-up of holiday protection in a generation. They are designed to give holidaymakers who book through online travel agents the same safeguards as traditional package holidays.

Simon Calder has been studying the new rules – and assessing the impact on Day One.

Q What problems are these rules solving?

Proper package holidays are the gold standard of travel. By booking flights and accommodation in a single transaction from a tour operator, you transfer all the risk to the company. A cancelled flight or an overbooked hotel? They have to sort it out, and provide a refund or compensation as appropriate.

But with the growth of online travel agents, people have been buying what they think is a package holiday, only to discover when it all goes wrong that the travel firm denies all responsibility.

It's summed up with the case of a couple called Chris and Janette from Perthshire, who contacted me from Croatia a couple of days ago to say they had turned up at their holiday hotel in Mali Losinj only to find it has been closed since Christmas.

If it had been a proper package holiday, the travel firm would have needed to run around and find an alternative immediately, and/or pay compensation. As it was, they called their online travel agent only to be told: 'Haven't you read the small print? Your contract is with the supplier of that product, which is a hotel booking service. So sort it out with them.'

Q What has changed?

The basic rule is now common to all channels of booking: if it looks like a package holiday, with flights, accommodation and possibly a rental car all included in a single transaction, then it has all the prodigious consumer protection that comes with a proper package.

The Government reckons the change could bring valuable extra protection to as many as ten million British holidaymakers.

Q What are the travel agents saying?

Leading companies have changed their terms to reflect the new rules with varying degrees of enthusiasm. On the Beach, one of the biggest firms, says very directly: 'On the Beach will be fully responsible for the proper performance of the package as a whole.

'Additionally, as required by law, On the Beach has protection in place to refund your payments and, where a flight is included in the package, to ensure your repatriation in the event that it becomes insolvent.'

Travel Republic, part of the Emirates Group, acknowledges it may be obliged to pay compensation, provide assistance or make alternative travel arrangements, saying: 'We do so because we are obliged to do so [by the new rules], not because we have a contract with you to supply those arrangements.'

But Sunshine.co.uk appears not to have updated its terms and conditions. After the new rules took effect, the company was still saying: 'Sunshine, because we act as booking agent, accept no responsibility or liability for the acts or omissions of, or services provided by, Travel Suppliers.

'We neither arrange nor combine nor package... travel products.' But whatever the terms say, online travel agents which sell flights and accommodation in a single transaction are obliged to provide assistance and, if appropriate, compensation when travel arrangements go wrong.

Q Are there any loopholes?

Yes. The new rules introduce the concept of 'Linked Travel Arrangements,' which provides much weaker consumer protection – basically there's no improvement from the old rules. Typically a Linked Travel Arrangement involves buying a flight and accommodation in separate transactions with separate payments, or – after buying one element, such as transport – clicking through to book another travel product.

Agents are obliged to specify if they are offering Linked Travel Arrangements. Just in case they forget, the key issue is: if you're asked to pay separately for flights and accommodation, there's a good chance you won't get any extra protection.

Q What do the holiday companies say about the new rules?

The whole industry is quite cross, because this is an EU directive which was issued in 2015, but the actual British law was only revealed ten weeks ago – which hasn't given them long to comply with the changes.

Online travel agents say their additional obligations will increase their costs and push up holiday prices.

One controversial element of the new rules is that holidaymakers have a new right to cancel with a full refund in the event of 'unavoidable and extraordinary circumstances occurring at the place of destination or its immediate vicinity and which significantly affect the performance of the package, or the carriage of passengers to the destination'.

There's no clear definition of what that might mean – for example if, heaven forbid, there were a terrorist attack in a resort 40 miles from the one you're booked in, it is not certain whether you would have the right to cancel if you decided you did not want to go ahead with the holiday.

Q Many people will have booked summer holidays through online travel agents before today but are going to travel this month or next. Are they now covered?

No, the new law does not apply retrospectively to existing bookings, which will lead to some odd situations. Suppose you booked through an online travel agent before 1 July for a hotel that turns out to be closed. When you call to complain the firm can just shrug. But if I book the same deal today, the online travel agent must solve the problem and pay appropriate compensation.

If you are a complete DIY holidaymaker, who finds flights direct from an airline, books a hotel independently, then nothing changes; the only protection you may have is from your travel insurance or credit card provider.

Q These rules come from an EU directive. Do they apply beyond Europe? And will they continue after Brexit?

They apply to holidays organised by any company in the European Union for travel worldwide. It is not clear if, after Brexit, it will apply to British holidaymakers who book with a firm based in the EU. But for trips booked through UK firms, the regulations are now enshrined in UK law and will continue in force after Brexit.

1 July 2018

EU plans to give consumers more rights against big companies

Consumers will be allowed to take collective legal action when wronged.

By Jon Stone

EU consumers will get more powers to challenge big companies in the courts, and a right to clearer information about who they are buying from, under proposals unveiled by the European Commission on Wednesday.

The new package of measures comes on the heels of the Dieselgate scandal, that saw consumers sold cars that emitted up to 40 times more toxic fumes in real-world driving than claimed.

Under the proposals, consumer groups would gain powers to sue large corporations for collective redress on the behalf of those affected by such unfair commercial practices.

Penalties for firms that break the law would also be increased, with a maximum fine of at least 4% of the trader's annual turnover in any given member state – and national governments allowed to go higher if they want.

British consumers could miss out on the new rights if they are only finalised after the Brexit transition period – though the UK has agreed to implement all new EU rules that come into force before 2021.

'In a globalised world where the big companies have a huge advantage over individual consumers we need to level the odds,' Věra Jourová, Commissioner for Justice, Consumers and Gender Equality said.

'Representative actions, in the European way, will bring more fairness to consumers, not more business for law firms. And with stronger sanctions linked to the annual turnover of a company, consumer authorities will finally get teeth to punish the cheaters. It cannot be cheap to cheat.'

The so-called New Deal For Consumers package would also attempt to bring more transparency to online market places and shopping search engines. The Commission wants such websites to label clearly whether an item is being sold by a trader or private person – so consumers know whether they are covered by protections.

European Commission first vice-president Timmermans said: 'Today's New Deal is about delivering a fairer Single Market that benefits consumers and businesses.

'We introduce a European collective redress right for when groups of consumers have suffered harm, like we have seen in the recent past, with proper safeguards so there can be no misuse. Consumers will know who they are buying from online, and when sellers have paid to appear in search results.

'The majority of traders who play fair will see burdens lifted. The handful of traders who deliberately abuse European consumers' trust will be sanctioned with tougher fines.'

11 April 2018

Ethical and Sustainable Trends 2019

by Sian Conway

2018 felt like the first year where ethical living really went mainstream. Major fashion magazine *Elle* dedicated their most important issue of the year, the September Issue, to sustainable fashion, and issues from plastic pollution to palm oil have dominated the news headlines.

Last year I made my predictions for the ethical and sustainable trends to watch in 2018, including plastic pollution, the rise of veganism, major growth in ethical fashion and a bigger push against climate change.

After reviewing the data from 2018, it's clear that significant progress was made in all of these areas, but these issues aren't going away any time soon.

Keeping up to speed with the latest consumer and market trends is essential for any business wanting to thrive in their industry, and understanding the influencing factors behind customer behaviour can help identify new opportunities.

So what ethical and sustainable trends can we expect to see in 2019?

The war on plastic continues, and becomes more complex

2018 saw our consumption of, and reliance on, plastic come into question in a big way. Since *Blue Planet II* first brought the issue into our living rooms, we've seen consumers start to question and challenge brands on their packaging, governments make moves to implement bans on single-use plastics and everyday behaviour start to change.

However, change takes time, and plastic is such a widely used, affordable material, it's unlikely that this problem will be solved overnight.

2018 saw an increase in bring-your-own cup schemes and extensive plastic straw bans. The reusable bottle industry is now worth £5.5 billion and the global market is expected to expand at 3.6% Compound Annual Growth Rate (CAGR) from 2017 to 2025.

'Single-use' was even named word of the year 2018 by *Collins Dictionary* and, according to sustainablebrands.com, online searches for 'plastic recycling' increased by 55% last year.

One million plastic bottles are still purchased around the world every minute, and it's predicted that figures will rise by another 20% by 2021 (according to refill.org), so there's still a lot of work to be done.

However, many conscious consumers have now made the simple switches – also known as the 'Big 4': drinking straws, takeaway coffee cups, plastic water bottles and plastic shopping bags.

In 2019 we can expect consumers to be looking for deeper, systematic change around single-use plastic.

This may lead to a growth in recycling schemes, but we can also expect to see consumer pressure pushing legislation and corporations to go deeper than that.

Leading market research organisation Mintel have named 'Rethink Plastic' as one of their key trends to watch in 2019, finding that 49% of UK consumers who already recycle most food packaging say that clearer instructions on which parts of packaging can be recycled is needed, and 71% of UK household care product buyers agree that using recovered ocean plastic in packaging is a good way to protect the environment.

We can expect to see more consumer pressure, resulting in more innovative solutions to alternative packaging and a circular economy for plastic waste.

Zero-waste shopping

In the fight against single-use plastic, customers are turning to zero-waste shops, and now it feels like almost every town has one.

They often stock a range of dry goods from pasta, to spices, tea, coffee and loose fruit and vegetables, alongside bulk household cleaning goods like washing-up liquid and laundry detergent for consumers to fill their own containers.

This is a return to the way we shopped before supermarkets, and whereas for the past few years 'zero-waste living' was seen as the latest Instagram trend for the privileged influencers able to fit their entire year's trash in an on-trend mason jar, it's now moving into the mainstream.

Some supermarkets have announced plans to ditch plastic packaging in their own-brand products, and Britain's first plastic-free zone recently opened in a supermarket in North London, but as consumers continue to embrace zero waste, the bigger brands are going to have to move faster if they want to compete.

It's possible we'll see an increase in shopping locally as the zero waste market continues to grow.

Renewable energy continues to rise

2018 saw big shake ups in the energy sector, as UK consumers have continued to move away from bigger providers in search of a cheaper deal. Energy regulator Ofgem found that the big six had a net loss of around 1.4 million customers between June 2017 and June 2018.

25% of consumers now use small or medium-sized providers (up from 19% of gas customers and 18% of electricity customers in 2017).

The main reason behind these switches may be financial, but it presents an exciting opportunity for smaller firms supplying renewable energy.

One such supplier, Bulb, have increased customer numbers to 870,000 since it launched in 2015 and their 2017/18 financial report is set to show a 1,700% increase in revenue from £10 million to £183 million. They have also been named as the UK's fastest-growing private company.

Around the world, China has already surpassed its 2020 solar panel target and is expected to exceed its wind target in 2019, making them the world's renewable growth leader and putting them on track to account for over 40% of the total global clean energy mix by 2022.

India is expected to more than double renewable capacity by 2020, at a growth rate which is expected to be higher than the European Union.

Rising consumer awareness, a growing sense of urgency around climate change, along with a range of new, competitive renewable energy providers to choose from, means we are likely to see more households switching to green energy in 2019.

Innovations in eco-friendly materials

From building materials, to pineapple and mushroom leathers and 'vegan meat', we're constantly seeing new innovations designed with sustainability in mind.

With the environmental credentials of the fast-fashion industry being called into question by the UK Government at the end of 2018, it's likely that we'll see more growth in innovative new fabrics that reduce the carbon footprint of our clothes in the year ahead.

In the food sector, there is growing demand from the UK's estimated 22 million 'flexitarians' for innovative new meat substitutes.

Tesco have already launched the UK's first plant-based steak which looks authentically pink in the middle after cooking, and US brand Beyond Meat plans to roll out their plant-based burgers, which go brown on the outside and pink on the inside when cooked, across 50 countries and six continents.

According to the Vegan Society more than half of UK adults are adopting vegan buying behaviour. Whether they're motivated by animal welfare or the carbon footprint of animal agriculture, the growth in ethical eating will continue to have a knock-on impact in the food sector and beyond, as people opt for vegan fashion and beauty products to match their lifestyle.

We can't predict exactly what will happen in the ethical and sustainability sector in 2019, but as ethical business owners, we can use our marketing, communities and collective voice to continue to campaign for change and move the needle for our cause.

As ethically-minded Millennials continue to increase their spending power, and issues like climate change continue to dominate news headlines and public campaign efforts, it's likely that the ethical market, and demand for eco-friendly products, will continue to grow.

The businesses that will thrive in the ethical economy are those with embedded ethical and sustainable credentials across their entire operations, who keep up with ethical and sustainable trends and who understand the demands of the conscious consumer and are ready and willing to meet them.

20 December 2018

Consumption: our position

It's good to enjoy food, clothes and treating ourselves. But the huge pressure to overconsume (and waste) so much is harming nature and people: Friends of the Earth's position.

We often buy things not because we need them, but because it makes us feel good and expresses who we are. We do need to consume stuff to survive and enjoy life, but excessive consumption is damaging the environment and harming people. We need to reduce overconsumption by doing more with what we have (e.g. by sharing, making better products, developing a circular economy), changing how we market and advertise, increasing empathy towards others to encourage more careful consumption, and supporting ways of expressing who we are that don't involve excessive consumption (e.g. through sports).

Facts about consumption

1. **What we think of as modern consumerism in the UK dates back to the 18th century and the explosion in the number of businesses using what are now familiar marketing methods.** By offering credit schemes and placing adverts in weekly newspapers, for example, shops began to attract and create new customers keen to move up the social ladder. The trend was closely linked to rapid population growth, social change, a need for better employment and a huge rise in urban populations.

2. **From 1950, advertisers started to use television.** They'd learnt from the propaganda tactics of World War II. Using psychological tools to create desire and drive consumption, advertisers began to appeal to more than our basic needs: 'To ladies, don't sell shoes. Sell them sexy feet.'

3. **The EU could benefit by €1.8 trillion if it developed a circular economy that reuses and recycles resources** – as opposed to the traditional linear economy of make, use and dispose.

What do Millennials and Generation Z consumers want from retailers?

By Marjorie van Elven

Four generations of consumers coexist nowadays: the Baby Boomers, born between 1945 and 1968; Generation X, born between 1969 and 1983; Millennials, born between 1985 and 1993; and Generation Z, comprising those born from 1994 to 2002. Catering for the needs of younger generations is key for many businesses' long-term growth strategy, as Millennials currently form the largest generation in the US labour force. FashionUnited has taken a look at the latest research about Millennials and Generation Z to find out who they are and what they want.

They mistrust businesses and want to see them do more for society

Only 48% of Millennials believe corporations behave ethically and that business leaders are committed to helping improve society, according to Deloitte's 2018 Millennial Survey. The consultancy firm interviewed 10,455 Millennials and 1844 Generation Z respondents in Australia, Canada, China, India, the UK and the US. 67% of surveyors believe most businesses have no ambitions beyond wanting to make money.

An overwhelming amount of Millennials and Generation Z members (over 80%) consider social and environmental practices to be just as important as a company's financial results. Criteria deemed as highly important for the surveyors include: positive impact on society and the environment; inclusion and diversity in the workplace; job creation and career development opportunities for employees; and innovative ideas, products and services.

American footwear brand Toms exemplifies the kind of fashion company Millennials like. Toms is best known for their 'One for One' programme, in which a pair of shoes is donated to a person in need with every product purchased. "We're in business to help improve lives", the brand says on its website. According to a worldwide brand value index made by marketing agency Enso in 2016, Toms ranks higher than Nike among Millennials, even though the former is only a fraction of the latter's size.

Millennials still prefer computers, Generation Z is all about mobile

While both are believed to be 'post-PC' generations, older Millennials are more likely to buy desktop and laptop computers than any other age group, including Generation X and Baby Boomers, according to Deloitte. The consultancy firm says Millennials see smartphones and PCs as complements, not substitutes. A study about online shopping habits conducted by KPMG in 2017 corroborates this argument. They interviewed 18,430 consumers from the Baby Boom, Gen X and Millennial generations. Only 11 per cent of surveyed Millennials said their most recent online purchase was made via a smartphone.

But Millennials might be the last generation to prefer PCs. According to Pew Research Centre's latest report on teens, social media and technology, published earlier this month, smartphone access is nearly ubiquitous among

US teenagers, while having a home computer varies by income. A staggering 95% of American teens have access to a smartphone in 2018 (a 22% increase in comparison to 2014), while only 88% of them own a desktop or laptop computer. 45% of the surveyed teens said they are online 'almost constantly'.

They are getting more and more visual

While blogs, Facebook and Twitter dominated the social media landscape four years ago, photo and video-based platforms are taking the lead in 2018. Only 51% of respondents reported using Facebook in Pew Research Centre's most recent research with US teens, down from 71% in 2014. YouTube, Instagram and Snapchat are far more popular than Facebook among consumers aged 13 to 19, with 85% of Generation Z consumers using YouTube, 72% using Instagram and 69% using Snapchat.

As the last generation that has lived part of their lives in a world without widespread Internet access, Millennials are slower than Generation Z in using Snapchat and Instagram. Only 54% of Americans aged 25 to 29 are Snapchat users, while 57% of them use Instagram.

YouTube seems to be the safest bet for businesses looking to reach both generations via social media, as it is used by 80% of Millennials. Chanel is a good example of a brand that is performing well on YouTube: the brand's channel currently has over 1.1 million subscribers.

They enjoy shopping online just as much as they enjoy brick-and-mortar stores

One may be led to believe physical shopping is at risk, considering how much time Millennials and Generation Z spend online. But nothing could be further from the truth.

While these two generations are indeed savvy online consumers, they still enjoy shopping at physical stores. 48% of surveyed Millennials in KPMG's 2017 survey reported their most recent online purchase was from an e-tailer. However, the same research pointed out Millennials have a much higher demand for instant gratification than older generations. They are almost twice as likely to say they'd rather visit shops to get their product right away, rather than buy online and await delivery.

Another recent study carried out by behavioural marketing firm SmarterHQ in 2017 claims 50% of Millennials not only do go to physical stores, they actually prefer going to them as a primary means of shopping. Although more connected and more inclined to use smartphones, Generation Z isn't much different. A study released last week by commerce marketing company Criteo points out that 65% of Generation Z consumers dislike buying things without being able to touch them and 34% of them frequently research about products online, but buy them in store.

'While specific shopping habits may vary, Gen Zers are native omnishoppers who like to visit stores but still prefer to take care of their shopping needs online. In order to deliver a personalised experience on all touchpoints, brands and retailers need to employ a data-driven approach to connect Gen Z customers with unique, on-trend products,' said Criteo's Chief Strategy Officer, Jonathan Opdyke, in a statement.

7 June 2018

Fairtrade calls on more fashion brands to set a deadline to start paying living wages

To mark the launch of Fashion Revolution Week, the Fairtrade Foundation is calling on more fashion and apparel brands and retailers to set a deadline by which they will deliver living wages in their supply chain.

On the fifth anniversary of the Rana Plaza garment factory disaster in which 1,138 people died, Fairtrade wants the industry to pledge to end poverty wages and ensure a fair deal for the people who make the clothes we wear.

To highlight the issue a new video released today shines a light on the dark side of the fashion industry and aims to show how we as consumers can play our part in improving the lives of garment workers. It shows that despite spending £27 billion on clothes in the UK each year, it's very easy to lose touch with how much our clothes really cost to produce when retailers slash their prices and wow us with bargains, or when big brands charge more for their labels. But what is the real cost of our obsession for cheap fashion, and how can we make sure a fair price is being paid to the people doing the hard work so they can care for their families?

Subindu Garkhel, Fairtrade's Cotton and Textiles Manager said: 'Too many fashion brands and retailers are still just paying lip service for living wages to textile workers. Several have made public statements supporting minimum wage hikes, but none have published any tangible time-bound results showing their efforts to reach these goals, so these commitments are all shirt and no trousers.

'18 months since launching our Textile Standard and our accompanying Programme, we've learned that although it's challenging, it's possible to deliver transformative change to garment workers by combining a comprehensive on-site support programme for factories in close collaboration with local NGOs and trade unions.'

Fairtrade understands that certification and audits by themselves are not sufficient. Therefore it has developed an extensive textile programme, to complement the Fairtrade textile standard. This includes consulting and training at the factories and with workers with the help of local experts, training workshops and trade unions. Fairtrade Textile Programme also offers a dedicated productivity and efficiency training programme for factories.

Since the standard was first launched, much has been achieved in the areas of workers' rights awareness, strengthening their representation and capacity building of local trade unions and factory managers. With a mix of basic and advanced trainings Fairtrade has been successful in holding democratic elections at factories. Fairtrade also held several local workshops in South India and a session on Living Wages according to the Anker methodology last year. In addition, it has also carried out intensive research of the ginning sector.

A recent evaluation underlines the inclusiveness and empowerment of workers, trade unions, worker representatives or compliance committee members' participation in the audits and having the results shared with them. This sets the Fairtrade textile standard apart from all the initiatives out there.

'Brands and retailer can meet the demand for ethically sourced clothing by putting responsibility and transparency at the heart of their business, and a few have already begun to do so. We're calling upon the global fashion industry to turn its commitment to responsible sourcing into effective action by joining our Textile Programme.'

Suguna Ekambaram is a Fairtrade garment worker and is on the Environmental Committee at her workplace, Armstrong Spinning Mill, representing herself and the people she works with: 'If I have a problem I take it to the committee and I resolve my problem. If my colleagues have issues within the company they convey them to me, I take immediate steps to speak to the management to resolve the problem and we work happily. I am very delighted to work for this company.' The film will be screened around the UK by Fairtrade's vibrant supporter network, and taken up globally by other Fairtrade organisations, who raise awareness of Fairtrade and the trade justice issues which lie behind the Mark. The UK network of almost 10,000 groups is made up of Fairtrade Towns, Places of Worship, Schools, Universities and individuals who promote Fairtrade in communities and online.

23 April 2018

Can conscious consumerism save the world?

By Sian Conway

At the end of 2017, 15,000 scientists from around the world issued a 'warning to humanity' that our time is running out to tackle climate change. If we don't act soon it will be too late, and we're not doing enough.

The World Economic Forum's (WEF) 2016 Global Shapers survey gauged the priorities and concerns of more that 26,000 Millennials (age 18–35) from 181 countries. According to the survey results, the most critical problems in the world include:

- Food and water security
- Lack of education
- Poverty
- Climate change and destruction of natural resources.

Over the next few decades there will be a 'wealth transfer' as Millennials born between 1981 and 1997 will take over an estimated $30 trillion in wealth from the Baby Boomers and become the dominant spending power. We will also face some of the biggest global challenges as pollution, destruction of natural resources and climate change become even more critical.

A 2015 Global Corporate Sustainability Report by Nielsen found that globally, 66% of consumers are willing to spend more on products from a sustainable brand, with 73% of Millennials indicating similar preferences. (However, it is worth noting that several studies have also found that while consumers appear to be socially conscious in surveys, it doesn't always match up to their real-world behaviour, and cost, functionality and quality are still major factors in the purchase decision process.

The 2015 Cone Communications Millennial CSR Study found that Millennials are willing to make personal sacrifices to make an impact on the issues they care about. According to reports, this generation are switched on to social and environmental issues, willing to support brands associated with a cause and expect companies to publicly commit to corporate citizenship.

The soon-to-be global spending power are already 'voting with their wallets' and demanding more from brands to have a positive impact on the global issues they care about and are concerned by.

But can we really save the world by shopping with ethical businesses?

'Conscious consumers' are acting as agents of change by using their personal spending power to actively encourage brands that have a positive social and environmental impact, taking boycott or 'buycott' actions to put pressure on businesses to change their ways. Unfortunately, as brands have begun to recognise this demand and realise that consumers will pay more for it, we have seen a rise in greenwashing – brands investing money into marketing and PR activities that make them seem more green and ethical than they really are.

Confusing, greenwashed marketing messages and the overwhelming amount of issues can leave consumers feeling powerless and many critics of the conscious consumerism movement say that it's not actually possible under capitalism.

We live in a world where corporations can be more influential than governments and our political systems are often influenced by business concerns. It's easy to feel disheartened and many are left wondering – do consumers really have any power?

Journalist and sustainable lifestyle blogger Alden Wicker wrote a controversial piece in *Quartz* last year about why conscious consumerism is a lie. The article was met with mixed responses from the ethical and sustainable communities.

Alden argues that if we make small, everyday ethical purchasing decisions without questioning and challenging the larger, unsustainable corporate structures then we won't change the world as quickly as we want (or need) to. Although small ethical choices make the individual consumer feel good about themselves, it can serve as a distraction from the bigger picture.

(I don't think Alden is completely against conscious consumerism – but she recognises the complexity of the issue and the limitations of the movement. This piece on her blog EcoCult explores the issue in more detail and lists some ways we can all expand our influence further beyond just our ethical shopping choices.)

Tackling global issues like climate change, poverty and habitat destruction isn't going to happen in a vacuum – it requires systematic change.

Surveys have found that the introduction of the 5p plastic bag charges in the UK in 2015 have reduced single-use plastic bag consumption by over 80%.

Of course prior to the charges there were environmentally-conscious shoppers who declined single-use bags anyway, but it took a government-imposed, mainstream system to truly change consumer behaviour, break bad habits and change mindsets.

The Government have now announced their 25-year environmental plan which includes a pledge to eradicate all 'avoidable plastic waste' by 2042.

Many conscious consumers have been aware of the plastic problem long before *Blue Planet II* brought it to our attention and the issue went mainstream – but now there is significant consumer pressure on brands to ditch excess plastic packaging, plastic straws and explain why there is plastic in their products.

Major brands from Pizza Express to Marriott Hotels (who used 300,000 straws last year) have now pledged to remove plastic straws in response to this growing consumer demand.

The environment was identified by a Tory think-tank as the key issue for young voters – a major demographic that predominantly voted against them in the last election.

Plastic pollution has now become a major priority for the Government – in part probably to capture the interest of a younger, sustainably minded demographic of voters. Whilst this is potentially positive, there is a danger of it becoming 'political greenwashing' with no real, tangible impact – much like the greenwashing of major corporations.

Governments, commercial markets and consumer demands are inextricably linked, and to have real, meaningful impact, the whole system must be considered.

Ethics and sustainability are complex areas to navigate – often requiring compromise, extensive research and causing confusion at every turn. Living more ethically involves overhauling your lifestyle, one step, product and cause at a time.

Not everyone will become a 'conscious consumer' until the other options are off the table or it's the cheapest, easiest way to live. (Plus it's important to consider those that are unable to participate in the movement, for a variety of reasons; not everyone is able to participate as fully as others, as Francesca explores in this interesting and important article on her blog Ethical Unicorn.

Many conscious consumers are criticised for shopping at all – with the most ethical or sustainable option being not

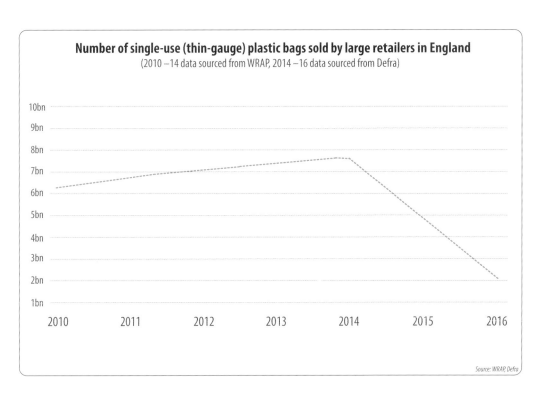

Number of single-use (thin-gauge) plastic bags sold by large retailers in England
(2010 – 14 data sourced from WRAP, 2014 – 16 data sourced from Defra)

Source: WRAP, Defra

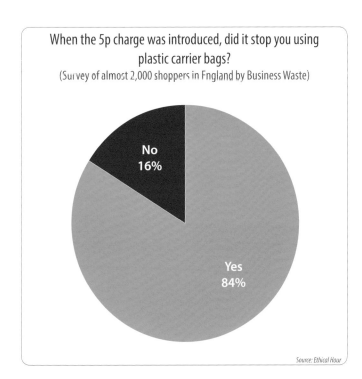

When the 5p charge was introduced, did it stop you using plastic carrier bags?
(Survey of almost 2,000 shoppers in England by Business Waste)

No 16%

Yes 84%

Source: Ethical Hour

The Oxfam multinational brand chart – these 10 companies own most of the food and drink brands in our supermarkets.

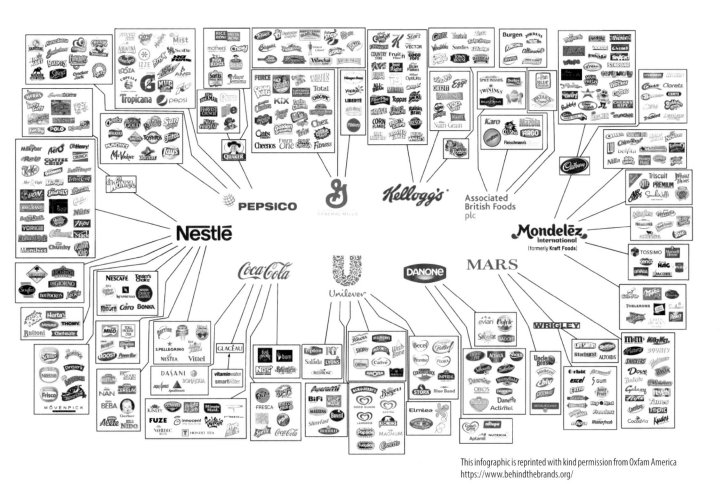

This infographic is reprinted with kind permission from Oxfam America
https://www.behindthebrands.org/

to buy something new, but to reduce, repurpose or repair instead. Of course this is the case but it's not always the most realistic option, depending on your lifestyle.

The first part of being a conscious consumer is about questioning whether you need to make the purchase and if no other alternative is available, finding the most ethical and sustainable option.

The driving force of commerce is supply and demand and while we live under capitalism, commerce is king. The Green Stars Project has written an interesting response to the claim that 'conscious consumerism isn't possible under capitalism' – challenging the often cited view that almost everything is controlled by just a few global corporations.

It's true that several major companies control the majority of the market in many cases, but social enterprises and ethical alternatives do exist – and as Green Stars points out, the fact that these responsible companies are usually in the minority is exactly why consumers need to support them.

Conscious consumerism grows the market share for ethical alternatives and demonstrates the much-needed demand that businesses respond to.

As an individual, making more conscious purchasing decisions can feel empowering and it's usually the first step people take into a more sustainable, ethical lifestyle. It's

not a simple issue and there are (rightfully) many questions about how elitist the movement is and indeed how much of an impact it is really having.

However, if conscious consumerism is the starting point to engaging people in a wider conversation, community and force for good, then it is having a positive effect.

We're at a tipping point with several global issues that will require drastic action, quickly and on a major scale. Small, individual changes are the first step to becoming a more mindful, socially conscious society.

It can be easy to feel powerless in the face of major issues. Often we don't care about a cause until it's too close to home, and by then it's often too late. If we are going to create a meaningful change in the face of these global challenges, we need to work together as a society. Governments and businesses will respond to consumer demand, so it is our choices and actions as conscious consumers that have the power to truly impact change.

11 February 2019

Ethical Consumer Markets Report 2018

The Ethical Consumer Markets Report has been acting as an important barometer of UK spending since 1999. We track sales data across a wide range of consumer sectors. The report is trusted and used by businesses, academics and the UK Government.

Executive summary

This year's *Ethical Consumer Markets Report* shows that governmentmeasures have slowed green spending, even as more consumers attempt to improve the sustainability of their purchasing. Government changes to taxation and subsidies have caused the collapse of two key green markets. Falling sales for solar panels and energy-efficient cars accounted for the slow growth seen by the ethical market overall which, at +2.5%, was outstripped by inflation in 2017.

Green spending

In many sectors, consumers are turning towards more sustainable options as their concern for the environment grows. Green energy grew an impressive 56.3% in 2017. Ethical clothing increased by 19.9% and buying second-hand clothing for environmental reasons increased 22.5%, in a year which saw much media attention about the environmental impacts of fast fashion.

Ethical Food and Drink was also up 16.3%, the largest increase since 2012, fuelled by growing sales of vegetarian products. The strength of such spending is remarkable since

UK retail sales fell in 2017 for the first time since 2013 and have remained challenging since. Our YouGov survey also exposed growing environmental concern. Over a quarter of those who responded to our YouGov survey stated that they had avoided buying a product or using a service due to its negative environmental impact in the past year – an increase of 65% since 2016.

Government cuts

Yet this drive for green options was offset by the removal of government support for green spending. Sales of solar panels fell by 87.4% in 2017 after the government reduced support for at-home solar energy generation.

The market for energy-efficient cars also fell 28.4%, following changes to road taxation.

In 2016, the Government cut incentives for solar panels, known as Feed-In Tariffs (FITs), by 65% and, in 2017, it ended subsidies for solar thermal schemes.[1]

The market has been declining ever since and, in 2017, it was less than a quarter of its 2010 size, when FITs were first

Ethical spending in the UK, 2000 – 2017

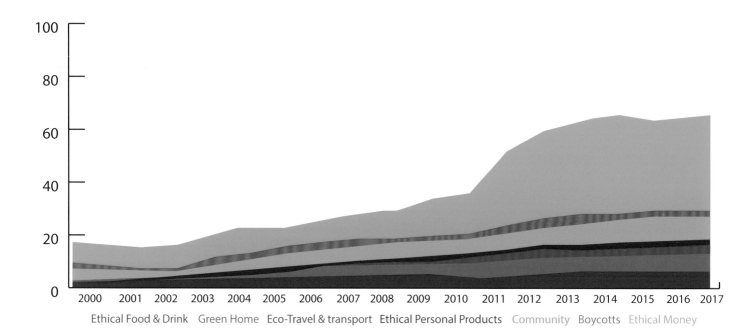

Ethical Food & Drink   Green Home   Eco-Travel & transport   Ethical Personal Products   Community   Boycotts   Ethical Money

introduced. As of April 2017, the government also changed its rules on road taxation. The new rules leave buyers of fuel-efficient cars £140 worse off after the first year than under the previous regulations. Encouragingly, however, sales of alternative fuel vehicles (pure electric and hybrid vehicles) continued to grow. Pure electric vehicles were not affected by the changes in taxation. The impact of such changes on the market as a whole is apparent. If the decline in solar panel sales and energy efficient cars is excluded, growth in ethical spending looks healthy at 5.5%.

The UK government's removal of financial incentives around renewable energy installations and lower-impact cars shows that we currently have a regulator choosing not to help ethical markets.

Average Ethical Spend

(£ per household, per year)

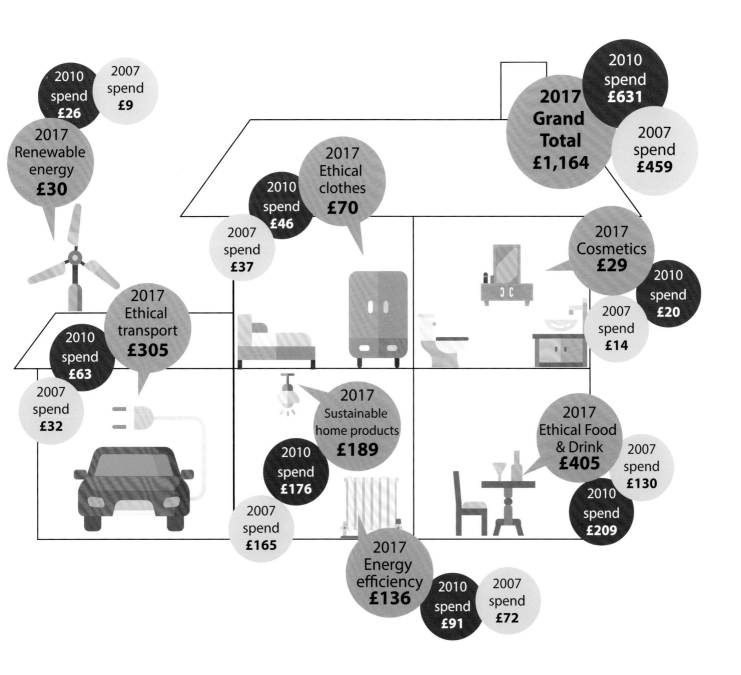

Consumer opinion survey

The *Ethical Consumer Markets Report* combines market-size measurement with a YouGov opinion survey of general ethical consumer behaviours. We ask respondents a series of questions about their shopping habits. The results of this survey are freely available on the Ethical Consumer website.

All figures (not market size calculations), unless otherwise stated, are from YouGov Plc. Total sample size was 2,017. Fieldwork was undertaken between the 24 and 25 of October 2018. The survey was carried out online. These figures have been weighted and are representative of all UK adults (aged 18+).

Personal boycotts

Many large campaign groups have moved away from the use of boycotts as a campaign tool and towards supporting accreditation schemes like Fairtrade and the Marine Stewardship Council. Despite this, much of the UK population are currently operating personal boycotts over ethical issues.

According to our survey, at least 49% of the UK population have chosen not to buy a particular product or shop at a particular outlet because of concerns about its ethical reputation.

The most popular types of personal boycott operated by shoppers in the UK, in October 2018, were against businesses with poor animal welfare standards (31%), a negative environmental impact (27%) and unethical corporate practices (19%).

Since 2016, there has been a 65% increase in those that have avoided buying or using a product or service due to its negative impact on the environment. Such growth correlates with increasing press around issues such as palm oil and clothing, and their impact on our rapidly warming climate. The number boycotting for political reasons has also increased by 67% since 2016, perhaps following high-profile boycotts around Brexit and businesses linked to the Trump administration.

When consumers who claimed to boycott were asked which issues drive their decisions, their replies were as shown in the chart below:

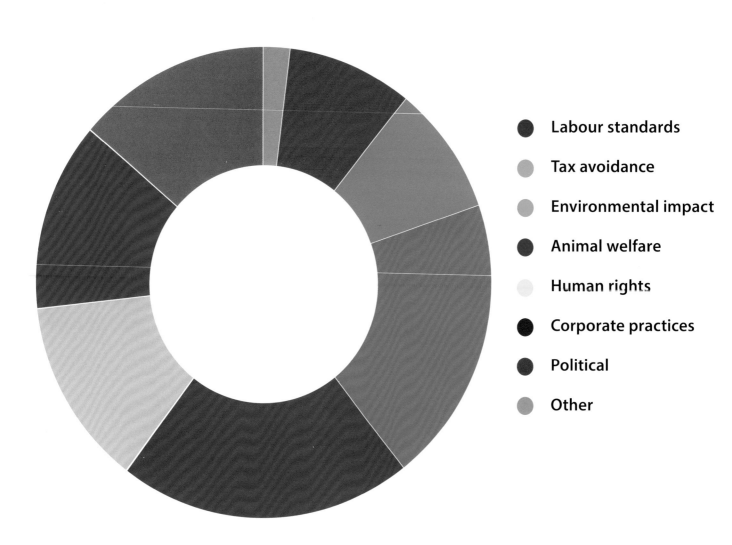

- Labour standards
- Tax avoidance
- Environmental impact
- Animal welfare
- Human rights
- Corporate practices
- Political
- Other

Ethical diet choices

At least 64% of those who answered our survey said they had made specific decision about their diet in the last year because of environmental or animal welfare concerns.

Since 2016, the number of vegetarians has increased by 52% and the number of vegans by 153% (although still only accounting for 11% and 3% of the population, respectively). It is also worth noting significant year-on-year increases in the number of people avoiding red meat and choosing fish over meat since 2016 of 54% and 44%, respectively.

The table below shows that by far the most popular change remains buying free-range products, a finding in line with the previous section which highlighted animal welfare as consumers' number one reason for boycotting.

Results of the question, 'Which, if any, of the following have you done specifically for environmental/animal welfare reasons in the last year? (Please select all that apply)' can be seen in the table below.

Other ethical activities

At least 74% of respondents were doing things in their lives specifically for social, environmental or animal welfare reasons in the last 12 months, a small decline from our findings last year, but a 7.4% increase since 2016.

The decline is likely to reflect a return to more normal levels after significant rises in 2017. Prominent campaigns around plastic pollution, fast fashion and palm oil appear to have placed ethical consumption on the public's radar last year. Although some of this interest continued throughout 2018, our figures show the difficulty of sustaining momentum for more sustainable buying.

Below are some of the significant figures from these findings:

- 63% of people recycled at least every week. However, this was a decline from 69% last year.

- A quarter of the population are avoiding using private cars and choosing to walk, cycle or use public transport instead.

- The number of those that have done the following in the last year for social or environmental reasons has increased by 20% or more since 2016: talked to friends or family about a company's unethical behaviour; chosen to buy/use a product or service because the company has a reputation for being ethical; recommended a company to a friend or family member because it is an ethical company.

- Women were much more likely to conduct ethical activities than men, with 78% of all women surveyed stating that they had done one of the things in this category, compared to 70% of men, and outperforming on all answers.

17 December 2018

References: 1 https://www.theguardian.com/environment/2016/apr/08/solar-installation-in-british-homesfalls-by-three-quarters-after-subsidy-cuts; https://www.independent.co.uk/environment/solar-power-crisistory-government-new-installations-drop-80-per-cent-conservatives-solar-trade-a7682501.html

Which, if any, of the following have you done specifically for environmental/animal welfare reasons in the last year? (Please select all that apply)	2018	2017	2016
Avoided eating red meat	14%	14%	9%
Bought free-range meat or eggs	48%	52%	39%
Tried to eat fish instead of meat	19%	17%	13%
Not eaten any meat (i.e. I am a vegetarian)	11%	9%	7%
Not eaten any meat or animal products such as eggs and milk (i.e. I am a vegan)	3%	2%	1%
Other	6%	4%	3%

- In the UK, as many as 42% of British consumers are interested in a personalised diet based on their genes/DNA. (page 1)

- Spending data for the financial years 2015 to 2017 show that, on average, 15-year-olds spent £25.00 a week, compared with seven-year-olds, who spent £7.40. (page 3)

- On average, children aged between seven and 15 years spent £12.40 a week. (page 3)

- The 2018 Retail Sector report, titled *The Convergence Continuum* found that 74% of consumers still prefer physical stores compared to just 26% preferring online shopping, with 36% preferring shopping malls. (page 5)

- 95% of Brits know what Black Friday is. (page 10)

- The average British bargain hunter is willing to pay £300 ($400) in total for his/her Black Friday shopping cart. That is almost $115 less than American consumers, and almost $89 less than Canadians. (page 10)

- In 2017, Black Friday was the most popular in-store shopping event, cited by 77 million consumers according to the US National Retail Federations. However, Cyber Monday was the most popular online shopping event with 81 million shoppers, compared to 66 million online shoppers on Black Friday. (page 13)

- In terms of online sales in 2017, Cyber Monday overtook Black Friday in the US by $1.56 billion. (page 13)

- In the latest example of 'shrinkflation', Cadbury confirmed a number of its eggs were set to shrink in size in 2019. (page 14)

- Figures from the Office for National Statistics reveal that as many as 206 products were made smaller between September 2015 and June 2017. (page 15)

- According to reports by The Children's Society, families with children at secondary school pay, on average, more than £300 per child every year in school uniform costs. (page 16)

- In the UK more than four million children live in poverty. And research shows the impact of consumerism on teenagers is greater for those from lower-income families. (page 17)

- Recent polling indicates three-quarters (76%) of UK adults now use online marketplaces. (page 20

- According to Citizens Advice, more than 13,000 problems with purchases on online marketplaces were reported last year. Calls about problems with purchases in these forums have increased by 35% over the past four years. (page 20)

- The reusable bottle industry is now worth £5.5 billion and the global market is expected to expand at 3.6% Compound Annual Growth Rate (CAGR) from 2017 to 2025. (page 25)

- One million plastic bottles are still purchased around the world every minute, and it's predicted that figures will rise by another 20% by 2021 (according to refill.org) (page 25)

- UK consumers have continued to move away from bigger energy providers in search of a cheaper deal. Energy regulator Ofgem found that the big six had a net loss of around 1.4 million customers between June 2017 and June 2018. (page 26)

- Supermarket brand Iceland is driving toward a zero-plastic future pledging to remove plastic packaging from its own-label products by 2023. (page 29)

- In England, the 5p plastic bag charge in retail stores has led to an 85% decrease in usage. (page 29)

- 95% of American teens have access to a smartphone in 2018 (a 22% increase in comparison to 2014), while only 88% of them own a desktop or laptop computer. 45% of the surveyed teens said they are online 'almost constantly'. (page 31)

- A 2015 Global Corporate Sustainability Report by Nielsen found that globally, 66% of consumers are willing to spend more on products from a sustainable brand, with 73% of Millennials indicating similar preferences. (page 33)

- According to an Ethical Consumer Research Association survey, at least 49% of the UK population have chosen not to buy a particular product or shop at a particular outlet because of concerns about its ethical reputation. (page 38)

- Since 2016, the number of vegetarians has increased by 52% and the number of vegans by 153% (although still only accounting for 11% and 3% of the population, respectively). (page 39)

- Women were much more likely to conduct ethical activities than men, with 78% of all women surveyed stating that they had done one of the things in this category, compared to 70% of men, and outperforming on all answers. (page 39)

Advertising

Advertising is communication between sellers and potential buyers. This can be delivered via various platforms, including social media, radio, television, magazines, newspapers, billboards and website banners

Black Friday

Originating from the US, Black Friday is a global shopping event that takes place the day after Thanksgiving. Retailers drop prices to mark the unofficial start of the Christmas shopping season.

Brand

A product or service distinguished from other products usually marketed with a distinctive name, logo and reputation.

Consumer

A consumer is anyone who purchases and uses goods and services.

Consumer rights

A consumer has the right to expect certain standards in the goods they buy. The law says that the goods must be of satisfactory quality, fit for their purpose and as described. These statutory rights cover all goods bought or hired from a trader, including goods bought in sales.

Credit

A consumer can obtain goods and services before payment, based on an agreement that payment will be made at some point in the future. Other conditions may also be imposed. Forms of credit can include personal loans, overdrafts, credit cards, store cards, interest-free credit and hire purchase. However, reliance on credit can result in high levels of consumer debt.

E-commerce

Electronic business transactions, usually occurring via the Internet, e.g. purchasing goods online.

Economy

The way in which a region manages its resources. References to the 'national economy' indicate the financial situation of a country: how wealthy or prosperous it is.

Ethical consumerism

Buying things that are produced ethically – typically, things which do not involve harm to or exploitation of humans, animals or the environment; and also by refusing to buy products or services not made under these principles.

Expenditure

The act of paying out money.

Fair trade

Fair trade is about improving the income that goes to farm workers at the beginning of a supply chain, ensuring that they are paid a fair and stable price for the product supplied. Items produced using fair trade can be identified by the Fairtrade mark.

Gross Domestic Product (GDP)

The total value of the goods and services produced in a country within a year. This figure is used as a measure of a country's economic performance.

GDPR

General Data Protection Regulation is a privacy law providing guidelines for the collection and processing of personal information of individuals within the European Union.

Interest

A fee charged on borrowed money. It is usually calculated as a percentage of the sum borrowed and paid in regular instalments. An 'interest rate' refers to the amount of money charged on a borrowed amount over a given period. Interest can also be earned on money which is deposited in a bank account and is paid regularly by the bank to the account holder.

Recession

A period during which economic activity has slowed, causing a reduction in Gross Domestic Product (GDP), employment, household incomes and business profits. If GDP shows a reduction over at least six months, a country is then said to be in recession. Recessions are caused by people spending less, businesses making less and banks being more reluctant to loan people money.

Scam

A scam is a scheme designed to trick consumers out of their money. Scams can take many forms, and are increasingly perpetrated over the Internet: 'phishing' scams, where a web user is sent an email claiming to be from their bank in order to gain access to their account, are one common example.

Shrinkflation

The process by which a product's size is reduced while its price remains the same. Meaning consumers are paying more for less.

Assignments

Brainstorming

⇨ In small groups, discuss what you know about consumerism. Consider the following points:

- What is consumerism?

- What is a 'brand'?

- What do we mean by 'ethical consumerism'?

- What does the term 'materialistic' mean and how does this relate to consumerism?

- What are consumer rights?

Research

⇨ Conduct some research amongst your friends and family to find out what matters to them most when making a purchasing decision: brand, price, quality, company ethics? Write a report to analyse your findings and include at least three graphs or infographics.

⇨ Conduct a questionnaire amongst your class to find out how much people spend when they go shopping. You should compare and contrast the differences between males and females, and ask people about their online shopping habits as well as when they physically visited the shops. Write a report to analyse your findings and include at least three graphs or infographics.

⇨ In pairs, visit your local high street and count the number of shops that are vacant or closing down. Feedback to your class and discuss why you think high streets are changing.

⇨ Choose a brand that you are familiar with and research the techniques they use to encourage people to buy their products/services. For example, advertising campaigns, tie-ins with films or TV sponsorship, etc. Write a short paragraph summarising your findings.

⇨ Using the infographic on page 37 as a guide, have a look around your home and try to estimate your household's 'ethical spend' over the last six months.

Design

⇨ Design a poster that will encourage people to make ethical purchasing decisions.

⇨ Choose one of the articles in this book and create an illustration to highlight the key themes/message of your chosen article.

⇨ Design an app that will change the way people shop. It could be something that helps them compare prices, an app that tells you when you are near shops that might interest you or perhaps something that will help you find ethical alternatives for what you want to buy. Get creative and include sketches to illustrate your ideas!

⇨ Design your own product – it could be trainers, perfume or a soft drink, for example. Individually or in groups, create a 'brand' around your new product including a name, logo and a slogan. Think about who your product is aimed at and how you would reach that target audience.

Oral

⇨ In groups, discuss how social media puts pressure on people to consume the 'right' brands. How important is it to acquire the 'right' brands and why are they associated with achieving happiness?

⇨ Create a simple leaflet that explains your consumer rights when buying products. You should include information about digital content purchases.

⇨ In pairs, role-play a situation in which one of you is trying to convince the other to boycott a particular product or company. Think carefully about what you will say to persuade your partner and validate your argument.

⇨ Ask a relative who is older than you how they think consumerism has changed in the last ten years. Write some notes and feedback to your class.

Reading/writing

⇨ Write a blog post about the rise of mindful consumerism. Have you noticed your own consumer behaviour changing recently – if so, give some examples.

⇨ Imagine you work for a charity that promotes ethical consumerism. Plan a social media campaign that will encourage people to change their shopping habits.

Acknowledgements

The publisher is grateful for permission to reproduce the material in this book. While every care has been taken to trace and acknowledge copyright, the publisher tenders its apology for any accidental infringement or where copyright has proved untraceable. The publisher would be pleased to come to a suitable arrangement in any such case with the rightful owner.

Images

All images courtesy of iStock except pages 1, 2, 3, 7, 23, 24: Pixabay. 12, 13, 14, 15, 16, 25, 26, 28, 31: Rawpixel. 4, 5, 6, 17, 20, 27, 29, 30, 32: Unsplash.

Icons

Icons on page 10 were made by Freepik from www.flaticon.com.

Icons on page 11 were made by Freepik, monkik, Nikita Golubev, Pixel perfect and Smalllikeart from www.flaticon.com.

Icons on page 37 were made by Creaticca Creative Agency, Flat Icons, Freepik and Smalllikeart from www.flaticon.com.

Illustrations

Don Hatcher: pages 8 & 9. Simon Kneebone: pages 18 & 2. Angelo Madrid: page 33.

Additional acknowledgements

With thanks to the Independence team: Shelley Baldry, Tina Brand, Danielle Lobban, Jackie Staines and Jan Sunderland.

Tracy Biram

Cambridge, January 2019